Who could take anythi...
when we stride through the streets
with our hands held together?

mpT
MODERN POETRY
IN TRANSLATION
The best of world poetry

No. 3 2020
© *Modern Poetry in Translation* 2019 and contributors

ISSN (print) 0969-3572
ISSN (online) 2052-3017
ISBN (print) 978-1-910485-28-6

Editor: Clare Pollard
Managing Editor: Sarah Hesketh
Digital Content Editor: Ed Cottrell
Finance Manager: Deborah De Kock
Design by Jenny Flynn
Cover art by Lily Arnold
Typesetting by Libanus Press

Printed and bound in Great Britain by Charlesworth Press, Wakefield
For submissions and subscriptions please visit
www.modernpoetryintranslation.com

Modern Poetry in Translation Limited. A Company Limited by Guarantee
Registered in England and Wales, Number 5881603
UK Registered Charity Number 1118223

Supported using public funding by
ARTS COUNCIL
ENGLAND

Modern Poetry in Translation gratefully acknowledges the support of
The Writing Squad and everyone who contributed to our Indiegogo
campaign for this focus, whose names are listed at
modernpoetryintranslation.com

The Young Poets Network and *Modern Poetry in Translation* Challenge was
created in collaboration with the Poetry Society

THEPOETRYSOCIETY

MODERN POETRY IN TRANSLATION

Origins of the Fire Emoji

CONTENTS

Focus

Reviews

EDITORIAL

By Jasmine Simms and Helen Bowell, co-directors of Dead
[Women] Poets Society and guest editors of this issue's focus

How many dead woman poets have you read? Between 2008 and 2018,
only 28% of published translations were of women's work – and yet,
as you'll see in this issue's focus, there has never been a shortage of
brilliant women writers. At Dead [Women] Poets Society, we trace
the lineage between poets of today and their literary great-great-
grandmothers. Since 2015, we have 'resurrected' women poets at
'séances' around the country, working with contemporary writers to
bring more attention to poets like Anna Wickham, June Jordan and
Mina Loy.

We have loved guest-editing *MPT*. Translation is always a kind
of resurrection: translators by definition act as 'medium' between
poet and reader. But bringing anyone back to life is a risky business,
and is a power we must wield with care. In Bebe Ashley's kintsugi
constructed from Sappho's fragments, Sappho wonders how she
will be read and remembered in the future. When she asks herself,
'Sappho, who is doing you wrong?' we are reminded of the translator's
responsibilities, and the risks of misrepresentation, of 'doing them
wrong'. Suzannah Evans speaks to this, writing of Nadia Anjuman,
'I was keen not to try to speak *for* her at any point'. Meanwhile,
Rosanna Hildyard notes with irony in her introduction that Màiri
Mhòr nan Òran would not have wanted her work translated into
English at all.

But there are reasons to translate, and reasons to read works in
translation. Belinda Zhawi renders the story of an economic migrant
who returns an outsider, in her commissioned translation of Noémia
de Sousa's 'Magaiça'. 'I have become such a migrant,' she writes in her
introduction. It is that feeling of recognition, of *I am this, too*, that we
are hoping to find.

Women poets are often associated with tragedy. We wanted this issue to represent a diversity of women's experiences – both 'Gwerful Watches Her Friend Take a Shit' and 'One Hundred Short Tales of Cruelty' – and also a sisterhood. Ordered chronologically, the poets featured span four millennia and several continents, and yet they seem to speak to one another. We were immediately struck by the recurring motif of fire, from Jessica Wood's title 'Origins of the Fire Emoji', to the burning houses in Lakshmi Holmström's work, to Marina Tsvetaeva's image of a fizzing match and 'everything always | on fire'. We hope you feel, as we do, that this issue is also 🔥

We are beyond grateful to the individuals and organisations who contributed to and shared our crowdfunding campaign, without whom this Dead [Women] Poets focus would not have been possible. We are grateful, as ever, to our illustrator Lily Arnold for the artwork on the cover and interior, as well as to The Writing Squad, who helped to facilitate a translation workshop with young writers, and who have supported Dead [Women] Poets Society from the start. Finally, our biggest thanks go to the *MPT* team for so generously allowing us to guest-edit the focus for this issue, and holding our hands through the whole process. For 'who could take anything from us | when we stride through streets | with our hands held together?'

Love, fire and solidarity,
Jasmine and Helen
Dead [Women] Poets Society

HACHIKAI MIMI

Translated by Kyoko Yoshida

Mimi Hachikai is a prominent new voice in contemporary Japanese poetry and a recipient of many major awards. As a postgraduate student of Ancient Japanese Literature at Waseda University, she won the Nakahara Chūya Prize with her debut collection *Ima nimo uruotte iku jinchi* (1999), which was translated into English as *The Quickening Field* by Juliet Winters Carpenter. Ever since, Hachikai has been a prolific writer of poetry, fiction, children's stories, essays, and reviews. Her fifth and latest collection *Kao wo arau mizu* (Some Water to Wash My Face, 2015) covers private matters such as the death of her father and historic catastrophes including the 2011 Tōhoku Earthquake and its subsequent nuclear disaster. It attempts to reinterpret the present human environment as a 'hypothetical structure' that calls for fresh alternative visions. Simple everyday acts like washing one's face bear renewed importance in this context. Hachikai's poetry celebrates the primordial force of life found in humans and other lives, and explores the possibilities of subconscious memories beyond individual human experiences. In straightforward, effortless language, sometimes in dialogue with Old Japanese, sometimes with subtle humour, Hachikai opens up a textual space inside our bodies where poetic language regains its vivacious energy, just like she does with her pen name, Hachikai (beekeeper) Mimi (ear).

Byō Byō

It wasn't expected to be endless
But now at the dead-end, either onward or roundabout,
Onward or roundabout, rooted beings
Are growing near the field of vision.
At dead-end, they

Exist as they are to meet and
Bugle byō-byō, the blare of righteousness.
Righteousness, as a rule, comes with a tail,
And when stepped on, it bugles, barks, and bites.
Its mind becomes

Frail.
One wants to quit quarreling and leave the place
To wash one's mouth out.
In an age without example,
Minding the place where the dead gather,
The tails everywhere avoiding being stepped on, end up
Sweeping dust by their inherent moves.
Existing,
They are as they are to meet and to accept
The age's prospect.
The tail that barks when stepped on also
Grows on myself, and I catch myself
Sweeping up dust over dust.
Sweeping trails wide and narrow,
We bugle byō-byō
Into a fresh darkness, without choice,
To be reborn.

Let Me Switch off the TV

We hear the voice of the shackled from the bottom
Upon which we spread a dining table and eat our fried rice
    Never bothered by the invisible
        That's how the archipelago decays

We rush to the observatory
To observe a new explosion in the depth of the lenses
Just when extinction triggers
Generation of a next star

I spread a notebook and draw a winged being
    The dining table's legs grow roots into the soil
Into a cicada husk that I removed from a tree trunk and brought home
    I've buried myself for seven years
        Now I look for a tree to climb up
    The moment the husk sheds off
The face of the moon once stepped by the mankind brightens up
With his footprints still intact

MICHÈLE MÉTAIL

Translated by Philip Terry
Introduction by Michèle Métail

In France, around 1950, the 'Portrait-Robot' (the identikit picture) used by the police and the judiciary was invented. The combination of diverse elements is used to reconstitute the broad outline of a suspect's face. I used this title for a gallery of fifty portraits published in 1982, subtitled 'Mental imagery in the manner of Archimboldo and Nicolas de Larmessin'. For isn't language itself visual? Does not metaphor provide us with numerous examples of grafts which are on a level with the finest imaginings of artists? Certain words by virtue of their polysemy suggest metamorphosis, as soon as one plays with their literal and figurative meanings: the arm of a chair, the mouth of a river, the head of a nail...

To create its descriptions of people, this collection works with a simple principle: the assemblage of ready-made language, those fixed expressions cited in dictionaries, taken up in speech, repeated without a thought with only the slightest modification.

When, in 2013, Marseilles became the European Capital of Culture, I was invited to take part in a project. I took up the 'Portrait-Robot' again in order to send back to the people of Marseilles an image of themselves, as in a mirror. This series based on Marseilles was followed by others, this time in ten lines: Paris, Berlin, Vienna etc., which were collected in *Quelques Portraits-Robots en pied rehaussés de couleurs véritables* (Presses du réel, 2018). These are the texts Philip Terry has translated into English.

For public readings based on the book, lines are printed on coloured strips of paper, inserted horizontally in a frame. The individual lines are removed from the frame and dropped to the ground as the reading proceeds, symbolising the deconstruction of the portrait and the creation of a reservoir of phrases for a new assemblage. An endlessly open form based on combinatorics.

THE MASS TOURIST

NEITHER HEAD NOR TAIL
OUT OF BREATH
CURRENT AFFAIRS
NOSE IN THE AIR
UP AT THE CRACK OF DAWN
HEART OF THE CITY
CONTINENTAL BREAKFAST
HAIRY LEGS
CAMERA STAND
UNRESTRICTED VIEW

THE CAFÉ WAITER

GLASS EYE
WITHIN EARSHOT
NECK OF A BOTTLE
MOUTHWATERING
IMPORTED SPIRITS
LIP OF A JUG
FOOT OF THE TABLE
BITE OF A SANDWICH
FROG'S LEGS
MEASLY TIP

THE PAINTER OF MONTMARTRE

RED IN THE FACE
YELLOW-BELLIED
GREEN WITH ENVY
WHITE-LIVERED
GREY MATTER
BLACK LOOK
GOT THE BLUES
HAIR OF A BRUSH
FLESH COLOUR
TICKLED PINK

THE BOURGEOIS BOHEMIAN

JEUNESSE DORÉE
BALLETIC FIGURE
BEAUTIFUL TEETH
MOUTHFUL OF CANAPÉS
WITHOUT A LEG TO STAND ON
ARMANI
UNISEX
À BOUT DE SOUFFLE
VOICE-OVER
SKIN OF DREAMS

FEDERICO GARCÍA LORCA

Translated by James Byrne

Tomorrow, in a small coppice near the crematorium where his body
was cremated earlier this year in May, I am to scatter my brother's
ashes. He died at 46, at the height of London's pandemic lockdown in
April. The coroner reported a major heart attack, though we'll never
know if Covid-19 wasn't involved. He'd been ill for many years and
suffered with his mental health for most of his life, slowly slipping
through the net of 'social care'. And yet his death was still very much
unexpected, a major shock for the family. My brother (Robin)
loved poetry and, because he was also severely agoraphobic, when I
travelled down from Liverpool to see him, I'd often bring poetry
collections and drop them off at his flat in north London. The next
author delivered would have been Lorca and so, after wracking my
grief-addled brain before the funeral service, scouring for a poem to
read alongside the elegiac speech I was soon to give, it made sense
to look beyond my own language to Federico García Lorca.

   Lorca's *Canciones* (Songs) (1921–1924) are a collection of short lyric
poems, some of them offcuts or fragments salvaged from his previous
collection *Suites*. I imagine these songs a little like those of William
Blake's *Songs of Innocence*, in that they might be set to music or indeed
sung. Interestingly, perhaps not being able to fully face my brother's
passing, when I first translated 'Cancioncilla del primer deseo'
(Song of the First Desire), I changed it all to present tense (for
example, 'quería ser corazón', 'I wanted to be a heart', became 'I want
to be a heart' and so on through the first, second, fourth and fifth
movements. Fortunately, I was set straight by Katherine Hedeen
who – along with Juan José Vélez Otero – was helpful in sharing the
translational expertise from Spanish that I lack and, yes, waking me
up from an all too personal immersion into what was simply not there
in the original.

Tomorrow I will read 'Song of the First Desire' a last time for my brother, with an awareness of how tragedy and regret can, at times, both live in the past tense. Lorca's life was also cruelly cut short, at the height of his range as a poet, whilst hiding from Franco's fascist thugs. I will read the poem in memory of Lorca too, whilst acknowledging how different their lives were. For my brother, reading 'Song of the First Desire' again will, I hope, help to draw a circle of time. It is the moment to let his beautiful and tormented spirit be free.

James Byrne, 20th August 2020

Song of the First Desire

In the green morning,
I wanted to be a heart.
A heart.

And in the ripe afternoon,
I wanted to be a nightingale.
A nightingale.

(Soul,
spin orange.
Soul,
spin the colour of love).

In the bright morning,
I wanted to be myself.
A heart.

And, as the dusk fell,
I wanted to be my voice,
A nightingale.

Soul,
spin orange.
Soul, spin the colour of love.

VAUGHAN RAPATAHANA

Translated by Vaughan Rapatahana

This poem concerns my own continued angst at the loss of my son
Blake. He committed suicide aged 29, 15 years ago now.
I still miss him greatly and there is rarely a day that passes when I
do not think about him and about why none of his close family knew
he was so depressed as to take his own life. Me included, of course.
This mōteatea or song-poem is written in my own language te reo
Māori and, more specifically, is a maimai or loving lament, whereby
there is a repetition of a refrain and an accent on sorrowed
expressions. Translation being what it is, no measure of English
language competence can convey exactly the emotive meanings of the
Māori language version; there is a culturally nuanced divide between
tongues, or what Wittgenstein termed 'incommensurability'.

Finally, the origin of mōteatea was as a purely oral genre: they are
designed to be performed and accompanied by facial expressions,
gestures – and in this case – heartfelt grief. Somewhat sadly, another
meaning for mōteatea is grief.

No Primogeniture

o Blake
my lost son
where are you now?

it has already been many years –
like shooting stars
through my atrophic brain

o Blake
my lost son
where are you now?

all that remains
is this arrhythmic
obsequy,
an irregular
trebuchet
striking me
dolorous
every time.

o Blake
my lost son
where are you now?

I am reduced to
this anaphora:
I have nothing else.

NAI XIAN

Translated by Kevin Maynard

Nai Xian was one of several non-Han poets who rose to prominence during the Yuan dynasty (1271–1368). He belonged to the Karluk [or Qarluq] nomadic people, whose homeland was west of the Altai Mountains, though he himself grew up within China, south of the Yangzi river. His exact dates are not known. He died in an army camp far from home.

His poems seem to me to have that lightness and delicacy that one finds in the best (i.e. the most typically 'minimalist') classical Chinese poems. Of course for hundreds of years there had been many Han Chinese who took the culture of these 'savage' tribesmen ('lesser breeds without the law') as an opportunity for a poetic exercise in sophisticated exoticism; but here we have a fairly unusual instance of someone writing from inside that 'alien' culture.

Apart from the thoroughly conventional epithet 'jade-like' (literally 'jade very graceful'), what delights me is the specificity of the different furs (fox-fur and sable), the white wolf slung from the nomad's saddle, the breaking of the river's ice to water the travellers' camels, the poet's daughter's hat-pin either tipping out or breaking as she emerges from her wagon – both translations are possible... I've used the word 'snapshots', because that seems the best way to characterise this sort of short sequence of sketch-like diary fragments. Just as we today would use our smartphones to capture vivid memories of this or that moment on a holiday abroad, so Nai Xian uses poetry to arrest the flow of time and strengthen memory. But whereas our holiday snaps probably lack art, his poems have survived for six and a half centuries.

Five Poems from the Borderlands

1

clear autumn skies
    in desert dunelands
        pepper plant shrubs
            few and far between

coats of fox-fur
    sable caps
        go hunting
            circling round
bowshots bring down
    white wolves
        their carcasses now dangle
            from the nomads' horses

at midnight
    pipes are blown
        on their return

2

chaotic jostling
    of felt-covered wagons
        at least a hundred, maybe more
at the fifth watch
    plunging pell-mell
        through the snow
then they cross
    the river Luan

one old woman lugs her cart
        she knows this route so well
we lean down from the bank
        and crack the ice
                to give our camels water

3

my jade-like
        youngest daughter's
                twin top-knots:
                        so graceful ...
and, after rolling up
        the cart's front felt screen
                she emerges
suddenly she sees
        one branch of violet blossom

and snaps the hat-pin
        at her hat-brim's edge

4

mare's milk:
        fresh kumiss
                fills our bottles
rank smells
        of desert goat,
                ground-squirrel meat ...
and when we finish bellowing
        the 'Trampling Song'
                the whole camp's drunk:

a small drum thumps
  as we process
    beside the deep blue sea ...

5

Wuhuan tribesmen's camp-mounds:
    the rain begins to clear

purple of chrysanthemums,
   gold of lotus-blossom
festooning every corner of this land ...

and right beside my horse
   a pair of skylarks
     (by far my favourite birds)

        warbling as they fly

PATRICIA ESTEBAN

Translated by James Womack

One of the things that is most immediately striking about the poetry of Patricia Esteban is her attention to the edges of things, to those elements of a life, or a world, or in this case a piece of writing, that are so often overlooked, or ignored. We are used to hearing that poetry should in many ways be a form of attention, of intense looking, but it is rare to come across someone who applies that criterion to the tiny slips and spills within a text: the footnote symbols, the asterisks, the hyphens, the page numbers, all the conventions which we use to tell us how to read words on a page, or orient ourselves inside a book. These two poems are from a sequence in Esteban's first and so far sole collection, *El rescate invisible*, that plays with typographical ideas; another series of poems takes some of its inspiration from a child's drawing found in the street. Out of the ephemeral, the unnoticed, the abandoned, Esteban builds a sly and witty poetry, that slows down our reading, alters how we see and interact with the page in front of us.

Critically Endangered Species

Watch what happens when I reach the end of this line, on the word bo-
dy. Did you see that? You're looking a bit confused: OK, I'll go again. Bo-
dy... I guess I'll have to explain it: you've just seen one of the last exam-
ples of a critically endangered magic trick, an old favourite, cutting a bo-
dy in half without really severing it, the sword in this case being the hy-
phen which divides words at the ends of lines and which is being brutal-
ly eradicated and which we are here trying to save, because there is no-
thing like using our projective imagination to recover a previously guillo-
tined word, a task to keep us on tenterhooks as well as enliven vari-
ous types of reading, from ho-hum novels to technical reports, with ti-
ny jolts of suspense, the suspense peaking as you reach the next chap-

Don't Turn The Page

Dawn was breaking just keep reading, don't look up, most importantly,
pretend to be engrossed in these lines so he won't suspect a thing who?
you may well ask, and you will soon have an answer, but don't stop
reading, don't move your head, just listen: the suspect is the apparently
inoffensive symbol looking at you from down there, in the corner of the
page, no, I told you not to look, careful, not even out of the corner of
your eye, the number's watching you, he doesn't care about the critics
tearing their hair out over his lack of interpretative possibilities, he's
barely interesting to those scholars who suffer agonies over textual
relationships, but he's definitely going to be the protagonist of future
references, appearing after the abbreviation 'p.' for 'page', and he is lying
in wait and you are going to fall into his trap in just a few lines, now
you see what's happening: reader, cover your eyes and, like Ulysses,
ignore his insistent demands, hold back, turn back to the beginni

ABU AL-QASSIM AL-SHABBI

Translated by Ali Al-Jamri

'Speak to me, you, the darkness that consumes us, | can life return when the springtime of youth withers?' The question captures the personal and political anguish troubling Abu Al-Qassim Al-Shabbi when he penned 'The Desire of Life' in 1933. Personal, because Al-Shabbi was just 24 and dying of a heart ailment. Political, because he was expressing the bottled rage and resentment of Tunisians under imperial French rule. This is the heartbreak of an ambitious artist, bitter in the knowledge of his own mortality and his country's exploitation, channelled into his finest poem.

I translated 'The Desire of Life' with the aim of celebrating its thrilling, lyrical energy. The poem's opening lines compel the reader to action and echoes in the slogan of the 2010–11 Tunisian Revolution – *al-sha'ab yurid isqat al-nidham* – The People Desire the Regime's Downfall. This slogan was on the lips of millions of protesters, first in Tunisia then in Egypt, Bahrain, Syria, Yemen and Libya, and has been heard again in the streets of Beirut this summer. 'The Desire of Life' heralded a decade of protest bookended by the Arab Uprisings and Black Lives Matter.

Keeping the 'r' end-rhyme which runs through the original text was an exciting challenge. *Desire* trills through the original verse, opening one line to the next, so that the entire poem itself is like '*the soft beat of a wing | its lift-off in reach*'.

Towards the end of the poem, the above question to the darkness is answered by the arrival of Spring, who '*kisses the lips of departed youth | with a passion that restores their colour*'. Today's protests echoing Al-Shabbi's poetry are like Spring's kiss, restoring his memory to life, time and time again.

The Desire of Life

One day, when the People act on Life's desire,
they'll force the hand of a higher power,
Night shall flee at the sound of Dawn's choir
and the chain, the chain shall finally shatter.

> *For if the People do not thirst for life,*
> *why, they'll shrivel and expire –*
> *those who scorn the struggle for life,*
> *Death shall punch with the force of a boxer.*

So said Earth through her creations
when our sorry state roused the forces of nature.

From mountains, through valleys,
beneath my trembling feet, the Wind blasted his anger:

> *When destiny calls, I seize the day,*
> *warn me of danger and I'll shriek with laughter –*
> *I'll always take the path less travelled*
> *I'll always run through the blazing fire –*
> *if the view from the peak makes you tremble with fear,*
> *then crawl in a grave and await your maker.*

If all youth are like me, then their blood's run cold
and their heart's drummed to the beat of despair.
I slipped in the slop and the mud, assailed by rains,
attacked by winds, condemned by thunder.

Earth, you hold us in such contempt,
how dare you call yourself a mother?

I bless of your lot the children of ambition
who chase and snap at the heels of danger,
but I curse the louts who waste this gift,
who aspire to live the life of a boulder.
The Universe is alive! He loves the living, he scorns the dead.

Does the bee kiss the dead flower?
Does the horizon embrace the dead bird?
Does the maggot distinguish the great from the lesser?
Were it my way, my dear, I'd not allow for burials,
but my tender heart breaks for the weeping mourner.

Spread my warning to those who accept a life in fetters:
When their story ends, Death alone emerges the victor.

On an overcast night one autumn,
as I watched Earth's displeased clouds gather,
I raised my cup to see off the stars
and sang 'til Sorrow joined my stupor.

Speak to me, you, the darkness that consumes us,
can life return when the springtime of youth withers?

But the Dark's lips did not part,
nor did Dawn voice her bewitching murmurs.
It was the Forest who spoke, like a lilting harp,
so delicate, so loving, so tender:

Here comes Winter, the winter of fog
the winter of ice, the winter of downpours
to snuff the magic, the magic of branches,
the magic of flowers, the magic of nectar.
The beloved blossoms of youth and yearning
are thrust unceremoniously in the air,
whipped this way and that by the hostile Storm,
drowned by the Flood, they are torn asunder.
Like a dream illuminated by the soul
then blotted out, all, all expire.

But in the earth remains the Seed,
springtime's forgotten, hidden treasure.
Memories of seasons, visions of life,
ghosts of a world, its base and its tenor —
the Seed embraces them all, beneath dead earth
and thick fog, a shield against Winter's icy spectre.
It grips Life in all its thrumming joy
and bears the promise of Spring's green wonders.
It dreams of birdsong in flight,
the juice of a fruit, the scent of a flower.

Time marches on, with it an oppressor,
and when this one falls, there shall come another.
Dreams rouse from troubled sleep
in a twilight that will not disappear.
They ask: Where is the morning mist?
            The evening's spell? The moonlight's shimmer?
            Where is the singing bee and the passing cloud?
            Where does the elegant butterfly flutter?
            Where are all the Earth's creatures?

Where is the light and the life I yearn for?
I thirst for the sunshine dappled through the leaves,
I thirst for the shade of a tall tree's shelter!
I thirst for the brook between meadows
that tinkles and dances with the flowers!
I thirst for the bird's croon, the breeze's murmur,
and rain's gentle patter patter.
I thirst for the Universe! And yet, the world
I wish to witness, I must yet wait for.
For He, the Universe, is dormant, His grand awakening
on the horizon. Is it on me to make him stir?

This longing is like the soft beat of a wing,
its lift-off in reach. As it grows stronger,
the Seed breaks the earth and, peeking out,
beholds the world. No view delights it more.
Thus dawns Spring, the Melodious,
the Fragrant, the Inspirer of Dreamers,
He kisses the lips of departed youth
with a passion that restores their colour
and says to them: You have been granted life,
and the Seed has been your protector.
Bask in the Light that guides you, the restless youth
of this fertile land, to bloom together.
Whoever worships the Light in their dreams,
the Light shall bless them wherever it appears –
for you is this space, so radiant, so pure,
for you is this chance to truly prosper,
for you is all this resilient world's beauty,
so firm, so flourishing, so clear,

so spread as you wish across the fields
by your supple blossoms and sweet nectar.

And thus survives the breeze, survive the clouds
survives the moon, survive the stars,
thus survives this exalted existence and its allures
thus survives Life and its desires.

The Dark slips to reveal a deep beauty
which electrifies and inspires.
Across the Universe a strange magic spreads
willed by the wand of a master spell caster.
Incandescent stars radiate across the sky
and there spreads the scent of a fragrant flower.
A soul, strangely beautiful, flutters
on wings formed of the moonlight's shimmer,
and the holy hymn of life resounds
in a temple, bewitching every dreamer.

Across the Universe it is declared:
Ambition is the soul's triumph and Life's blazing fire!
When the People speak their spirit's ambition,
Destiny must bow to their desire!

The Young Poets Network and *Modern Poetry in Translation* Challenge

Introduction by Clare Pollard

This summer *Modern Poetry in Translation* was very pleased to work with The Poetry Society's Young Poets Network again, to set what we hope will be an annual online challenge. This year, in honour of Refugee Week, we chose a poem by Suhrab Sirat, a poet, writer and journalist from Balkh Province of Afghanistan who moved to the UK in 2014, and was recommended to us by Exiled Writers Ink. Suhrab generously provided a bridge translation of his poem from the Persian, along with notes, so that young poets could attempt their own translations or versions. In the end, from the many submitted, our favourite was this by Claire Carlotti, which we are publishing below. Suhrab's poem is a ghazal, a form with an intricate rhyme scheme in which each couplet ends on the same word or phrase (the radif), preceded by the couplet's rhyming word (the qafia), and Claire's translation seems to us the most elegant recreation of this, using unforced, clever rhymes ('unnnursed wounds', 'cursed wounds', 'rehearsed wounds'). There were so many other striking submissions though, from Crystal Peng's exploded ghazal, to Jhermayne Ubalde's free verse version in which 'the world sways on a bovine axis' – do look at the Young Poets Network website to read the runners up and longlist: bit.ly/ypnsirat

Translated by Claire Carlotti with Suhrab Sirat

Landscape of Wounds

I am the night; my soul, my gaze, my dream are the worst wounds
While in the shadowed mirror, my lips brush against pursed wounds.

Autumn bleeds through each season, my Libra upsets Sagittarius
And the arrow strikes Scorpio, releasing venom from burst wounds.

The bull, weary and mad, will shake my Earth, which his horns cradle.
This heart, stuck, is my donkey, crippled by unnursed wounds.

I have no sky in which to place my star, it drowns in dark;
I have no country, no land to make a grave for these cursed wounds.

Daddy leaves me dust and blood in the place of bread and water;
My school, which grew first words, now breeds first wounds.

Passion, logic have faded, just grey shadows in the fold
Of spirits, weakly dreaming, submitting to rehearsed wounds.

My name, my faith, my memories, even my words are scarred;
From beginning to end of this journey, I have always traversed wounds.

ILHAN SAMI ÇOMAK

Translated by Caroline Stockford

Ilhan Sami Çomak is a Kurdish poet who has spent most of his life in prison. Arrested in 1992, whilst a geography student in Istanbul, Çomak was tortured for 19 days before signing a false confession. He was tried by a military court on the charge of separatism for allegedly starting a forest fire in the name of the Kurdistan Workers' Party and was sentenced to death. He was 22 years old. This sentence was commuted to life and in 2011 the European Court of Human Rights demanded a retrial. The judicial panel gave Çomak another life sentence in 2015. Ilhan has just begun his 27th year in prison and has 4 years left on his sentence. Ilhan Çomak has written eight books of poetry whilst in solitary confinement. His latest book, *Geldim Sana*, (I Came to You) won the prestigious Sennur Sezer prize for poetry in 2019.

PEN Norway is leading a campaign advocating for Çomak's freedom. Translator Caroline Stockford is working with fellow translators on a collection in English to be published in 2022. An anthology is also being prepared of poems for and with Ilhan. So far poets Ruth Padel, Alice Oswald, George Szirtes and Michael Baron are among the contributors. Four Norwegian poets, along with Caroline Stockford and Menna Elfyn, are writing poems in collaboration with Ilhan. Çomak's poems have been translated into Welsh, Irish Gaelic, Norwegian and Russian. For more information and to write to Ilhan, visit ilhancomak.com

Things That are Not Here

There are no kids scaling back walls
to skip school. No human bond of good
making friendship from mere words.
There are no stones for throwing stones.
No flowers pooling dew, no rivers
overflowing the map. No fresh-baked
smell of sesame bread to summon up
a crowd. There are no women
of selflessness and beauty, no possibility
to stretch out on grass and test the
constancy of sky. There is no candle,
just as there is no lamp. No darkness.
There is absolutely no darkness.

There are no turnings of the seasons,
no eclipses of the moon. No earth,
no plants in their simple elegance.
No cat's paws, no sweat-drenched
headlong of a horse. No curtain
for breeze to lift, no mouldering
bunches of grapes.

Life; separated from the sun.
There's no direction here.
But there is a way out.
Always a way out.

CLAUDIA BERRUETO

Translated by James Byrne

I first became aware of the work of Mexican poet Claudia Berrueto when we were participants at the Buenos Aires Festival of International Poetry in 2019. Claudia read from her book-length poem, *Sesgo* (Bias), a series of short lyric bursts of great intensity. I immediately wanted to read more. Around this time, I was looking for poets who might be considered for a book of Latin American women poets which I was about to commission for Edge Hill University Press, in collaboration with Arc Publications. In translation and historically, I've found poets from the north of Mexico – where there is generally more poverty and gang violence – aren't always so obviously represented anthologically as, say, the poets from Mexico City. Claudia's work published here is her first publication in a European poetry magazine of any kind (though I was pleased to note her poetry was included recently in the 'Crossed Lines' phonebook project, translated by Lorena Saucedo).

Claudia lives in the town of Saltillo, near Mexico's big city in the north, Monterrey, and is considered one of the major poets of Coahuila. She is a fellow of the Foundation for Mexican Literature and National Fund for Culture and Arts. Her collection, *Polvo doméstico* (Domestic Dust), won the national prize of poetry in Tijuana in 2009. The poems translated here are from *Sesgo* which won the Iberoamerican Prize Fine Arts of the Poetry Carlos Pellicer in 2016. In 2018, she joined the National System of Art Creators, and works, currently, as the editorial coordinator of Dissemination and Cultural Heritage at the Autonomous University of Coahuila.

Him

I

outside my house
the hoarse waters of early morning
parade through our lips

II

his eyes tiger through the kitchen
he explains the beheading of childhood
inside me
falling into the unborn excavation
of myself

III

the days rise like arrows of barbarous light
he bites and is torn away
and when he exits
i don't know how
split i am
which arrow i am

IV

for lou reed

we feed animals to live in the mind's zoo
then we watch a movie
but really
all attention is drawn to the sudden inclination
we have to breathe underwater
together

V

we take the road he drives
his voice clear as a glass of water
i drink and the clouds stare at us
becoming salt
even the stones evaporate
and the sky is a demented pet
who loves us

The Marvels Rest

and the moon moves the windows
i kiss your hair as if kissing the world's mouth
but the viscous voice of winter
asks me not to persist like the ant i am
asks me to stop dreaming
and with eyes blackened by sleep and rage
i still wish by your side
to burn the sky
to extricate one tear from the sea

Childhood

my dog transfigures into a corpse
i sleep with the anger of mud
chickens fall to the drain, flattened by my toys
a hundred sunsets laugh at me
trapped in the broken bone of a house
darkness running over my eyes
stagnated by a future, unarriving

THREE CZECH POETS

Translated by Matthew Caley

Much to my eternal shame – with a Czech wife and two bilingual daughters – I'm a very poor linguist.

This denies me the option of translation but forces me into writing 'the loosest of versions', using the crib of a literal or previous translation as a point of departure when I really have no right to. But it's the tension between unreasonable belief and perfectly reasonable doubt that make the poet, I guess. Hence these three 'versions' from František Gellner, Otokar Březina, and Karel Toman – all contemporary Czech poets. For instance, the Toman poem triggered strong recollections of my time living in Brixton squats. This collapsing of place and time, or the overlaying of one site onto another, is something I often do in my other work. The mind can be in two places at once, after all – and has to be in cases such as this. We travel between London and Moravia all the time. Though these three were written during Covid-19 lockdown – so perhaps I felt the need for an alternative mode of travel. I would never deliberately write a 'lockdown' poem but I do believe in a kind of 'parallelism' whereby, without direct intention, a poem can by tinted by context. I must here acknowledge Václav Z J Pinkava, on whose website I saw the original poems – and thank him for turning me onto some poets I had not yet discovered. Re-wiring these poems is the best way for me to get to know their work. And beat the travel-ban.

www.vzjp.cz/basne.htm

Terminal

after František Gellner [1881–1914]

firstly, if I'm lethargic it's from too much lethargy
and as for the daily grind – shove it!
O to dump the in-tray, this Doodle-poll, the out-tray
the terms and conditions, The Dow, The Footsy, the Excel-spread sheet –
      how I'd love it,
love to start afresh, a non-starter,
since incompetence is my skill, my USP.
This copy deserts its writer,
   my hand suffers repetitive strain injury

  suffers repetitive strain injury   but here's a fact:
if I were a woman
   I'd meet the city done up with *Rimmel* and khol

   as if I couldn't be fucked
about anything, my mini hoiked, all tush and tan
   happy to sell my body and my soul.

Simulacra

after Otokar Březina [1868–1929]

secondly – sat on a window-sill I rolled a *Rizla* then lit
an infinity cigarette,
dust, lint and smoke-scent crowning my head
as random images drifted
up and amongst them. But then these dust-motes,
as if the swirl of a screen-saver, shape-shifted
into the form of a smiling Fly-girl
 with sable locks, a come-on pout,
   a form which strained

 against enslaving lace.
How I wanted to kiss,
 then kiss again that wanton face

 and body, through head-spin and ganja-psychosis.
I blew the smoke but bliss
 disappeared. Only the bright cul-de-sac met my eyes.

The Weather Vane

after Karel Toman [1877–1946]

    thirdly, a dilapidated squat. in the wall-
cracks creeping moss, dewlapped mushrooms, tick-infested lichen chill
out or doze. In the yard
nettles hustle bindweed
in a tangle. The ornamental fountain that Lee
and Vags once fell in is over-run. The slashed tree
full of apple-blight and lightning
    that cannot remember when it was hung

    with blossom. Though on clear days, to be fair, linnets
rustle and whistle and on sunny days
    the gable's weather-vane

    begins to spin in
time, its creak singing to the heat-haze
    somewhere between joy and pain. Everything
                       is camouflage.

ORIGINS OF THE FIRE EMOJI

Focus on Dead [Women] Poets

ENHEDUANNA

Translated by Jessica Wood

Enheduanna was a high priestess in the 23rd century BCE, elected to create calm and unity amongst conflicting groups of people in the Sumerian city of Ur, now southern Iraq. She is the earliest poet whose name has been recorded, with a legacy that continued long after her death. Her poem 'Nin-me-šara', known as 'The Exaltation of Inanna', honours the female goddess of war and sex who she turns to for strength and support after being exiled. This record of her faith, hopes and fears was etched onto wet stone and solidified for thousands of years, so that we can still enjoy and identify with her words now. In this translation, I was interested in drawing out the language and methods we use today to encourage and affirm each other, focusing on specific celebrity figures who could be considered icons of femininity and empowerment. In the present day, the equivalent of our praise songs are encoded through comments and likes, hashtags and emojis which are made to be shared in an online space. I'm interested in the community that can be built when women affirm one another and 'stride through streets with hands held together'.

Origins of the Fire Emoji

Beyonce, queen of all powers
Rihanna, goddess of success
Lauryn singing fiyah words of love
Cardi and Megan shining, resplendent with WAP.

Teach us, O wise ones, how to guard divinity
in our hands, down the length of our necks
into the thiccness of our thighs
and the soles of our feet.

Teach us how to entrance with exposed skin;
an eye glimpsing a bare leg, a low cut revealing
the dip and curve of breast, an arm stretched
above the head to show a soft spread of bare chest.

Teach us to laugh after wild cows in the field, to admire
the sun as she lights up a building we've seen a hundred times,
to fill the dancing places of our city, now overlain
as streets of praise to the enslaved.

Teach us how to sing a birdsong note of freedom,
to speak affectionately of each other into the dead
of night, singing hashtag praise songs:
#slay #yaaaassista #awholequeen

Who could take anything from us
when we stride through streets
with our hands held together?

Katie Byford by Lily Arnold

SAPPHO

Translated by Katie Byford

During one workshop for sixth formers, I described Sappho as 'the Beyoncé of ancient Greece'. Well, nearly: her words were memorised by thousands, sung far and wide for generations. She was adored.

These songs were committed to papyrus centuries after her death, probably by men; marred by time, those documents have been the site of countless disputes. Every line, nearly every word, needs an asterisk. No inch of text is neutral. Sappho, or *Psappha* in the dialect of Lesbos, is the original 'L/lesbian', a curio with many mythological lives, each retrofitted to the morals of successive generations. Unsurprisingly, she has become a symbol for womanhood, queerhood, to sing with a fragmented 'broken tongue' (frag. 31).

Fragment 1, known as the 'Hymn to Aphrodite', is the *only intact* Sapphic song known to us. Much of Sappho's renown rests on it. And yet translations frequently represent it as a misty-eyed love poem. The name *Psappha* lies at the poem's centre, but when we allow that poet and speaker are not the same, the 'hymn' reveals itself to be a curse. Obsession, manipulation and domination: this is the *eros* the gods offer, to which the woman is subjected *kouk etheloisa* (against her will). The joyless ending, *summachos esso,* makes no distinction between love and war. The queer voice calls out a violent trope in male poetry: if Psappha were a man, would we cheer him on in conquest? But there are no men here. For Psappha knows lethal desire lives in women, too.

Hymn to Aphrodite

I beg you   Love
    by your ken cut sharp & dazzling
       & your dread & deathless majesty
         & your finger-stitched tricks
child only to thunder   Oh fuck   I beg you do not
crush my chest beneath this weight   this sick twisted glut

Please   be at my side
        like the time once long ago
you caught a glimpse of my voice   a faint strain of song
& gave it your attention
      & abandoned the gilt
      steps of your father's house
      & came to my side

hitched a chariot   & magnificent bird creatures
  pulled you at a clip   round the world's dark curve
    thick-plumed beating down the vaulted sky split
       heaven down the middle

  & landed
     & with every blessing in your eye
a cackle lit the face that would never see death
 & you asked

What now   who's wrecked you this time
    what are you squalling for

Another deepest darkest desire
for the raving   raging will of Psappha
Tell me who I need to persuade this time
to take you back   Who   O
                    Psappha   has done you wrong

    Look   Easy
                    she ran before
                    now she'll run into your arms
    She rejected your lover's trinkets   expect as many from her
                    if she doesn't like you yet
    She'll adore you soon enough
                                    she'll have no choice

    Remember this   Love
come now   please
    help me in my sickness
    release the grip of it
        whatever it takes
                    to bring these longings to light
                    do it
    Let's go to war on this girl

SAPPHO

Translated by Bebe Ashley

Kintsugi is the Japanese art of embracing damage. Usually Kintsugi refers to the repair of ceramics with gold lacquer, where fault-lines and broken pieces are not hidden, but re-crafted into a close, and different, object. When I was reading about the subject, I couldn't help but think of Sappho, the surviving fragments of her work, and the poetic possibilities this collagist form could hold.

I wanted to retain Sappho's mastery of lyric in reassembling the phrases whilst producing something fresh in what is, for myself, a new approach to translation. By adding the anaphoric phrase 'Even in another time' to each couplet, I aimed to address the many translations of Sappho that have been produced in the past, and are still to come in the future. Sappho's work seems to transcend our temporal timeline in a way that very few poets have experienced. The phrase 'Sappho, who is doing you wrong?' refers to these multiple interpretations created but also to myself in questioning whether I have the authority to create this work.

Similar in approach to a cento, I stitched together the fragments of Sappho scattered in our books and across the internet to create new couplets. Therefore this poem was informed by various translations including those of: Michael R. Burch, Anne Carson, A.S. Kline, Richard Lattimore, Aaron Poochigian, Jim Powell, and C.A Swinburne.

Sappho, a Kintsugi

Even in another time, someone somewhere
will remember us.

Even in another time, sparrows stretch
over salt sea to the loveliest stars.

Even in another time, the dawn light scatters
your laughter glittering on this coal-black earth.

Even in another time, my wild soul here
like a hyacinth in the mountains.

Even in another time, I want to say something
but shame sends me stuttering.

Even in another time, Sappho,
who is doing you wrong?

Even in another time, I am weary
of your words, and your soft, strange ways.

SULPICIA

Translated by Julia Anastasia Pelosi-Thorpe

In whimsical scenarios typical of Augustan erotic elegy, Sulpicia subverts the genre's gender norms. Her male poetic love object, the pseudonymous Cerinthus, is at the heart of her poems. I've been intrigued by these six elegies ever since I first came across them as an undergraduate. Through the years, I translate and re-translate them.

The six are the only pieces generally attributed to Sulpicia, though her authorship remains contested. Long thought the work of contemporary poet Tibullus, the poems appear alongside his own, as well as those of other poets affiliated with the patrician Sulpicia's uncle Marcus Valerius Messalla Corvinus, a prominent patron of the arts in whose literary coteries his niece participated.

Only in recent years have readers begun to consider Sulpicia's elegies poetic creations in their own right, rather than autobiographical windows into Roman women's collective lives; or a universal sense of 'womanhood'; or a real-life, unstylised love story. The poems' grammatical intricacies are now appreciated more as artistry than as the naïveté of a 'feminine Latin' (Otto Gruppe, 1838) or the 'undeniably difficult' poetry of 'a very woman' (Kirby Flower Smith, 1913).

Poems 1–6

1

at last i have a boyfriend
>which would cause more rumours

if covered up (ashamed) than
>if stripped bare / begged by my poems venus

brought him forward placed him down
>in my lap / she

kept her promises i hope she or any
>body they call joyless

texts my joys / i don't want things tablet-encrypted read by no
>body before my bf / but i also like being bad

i'm sick of putting together a face
>they'll say i

was worth it with a man who
>was worth it

2

i hate my bday and it's here i have to
>spend it annoyingly rural sad

without cerinthus / what's funner than the city
>just how's a countryhouse or field or cold

arno river right
>for a girlfriend / messala ur

too obsessed w me
>relax

the roads aren't ready ur a harsh uncle / i'm
　　　　　leaving my mind and
emotions behind me here though u
　　　　　give me no choice

3

guess what
　　　　　the sad trip's gone from this girl's mind now her
bday can be in rome / we can all spend
　　　　　that day together
which now
　　　　　comes to u
who wasn't even imagining
　　　　　it could happen

4

great ur so sure in what u
　　　　　let urself get away with
it stops me
　　　　　suddenly
falling / u prefer wool-basketed whores to
　　　　　sulpicia serui /
people are stressed for
　　　　　me hurt i might
fall into a
　　　　　stranger's bed

5

cerinthus are u even being tender
        to ur gf
since heat now rakes my burnt-out
        body / ah i wouldn't
want to fight this sad
        illness if i
didn't think u
        also wanted this / but why would i fight it
if ur heart doesn't care
        about my pain

6

my light
    i hope i'm not as burning a worry
to u now
        as seems i was a while ago / since
i've never done anything i'd
        say i regret more / than that
last night i left u
        lonely
desiring to disguise my
    fire

FROM THE SUBHĀṢITARATNAKOṢA

Translated by Victoria Moul

These are four poems by women from the *Subhāṣitaratnakoṣa*, an anthology of Sanskrit lyric compiled around 1100 AD by a Buddhist scholar named Vidyākara. It contains 1738 short poems and extracts by over two hundred named poets (as well as a large number of anonymous pieces), probably dating mostly from between the seventh and eleventh centuries AD.

The anthology includes several poems attributed to women, four of which I have translated here: two by Vidyā (807 and 808), one by Śīlabhattārikā (815) and one by Bhāvakadevī (646). As far as I am aware, we know nothing of these poets except for their names; the form of their names, however, makes it clear that they are women. The Sanskrit text that I used is the edition of Vidyākara's *Subhāṣitaratnakoṣa* edited by D. D. Kosambi and V. V. Gokhale (Harvard University Press, 1957). The numbering of the poems is taken from this edition. I am also indebted to notes and translations by Daniel H. H. Ingalls.

Sanskrit poetry uses quantitative metres based on the patterned alternation of long and short syllables, similar to those of classical Latin and Ancient Greek. I have made no attempt to reproduce these metres in my translation, though the formal features of the translations, and the variance in form between them, is intended to reflect the metrical constraints of the originals. As Sanskrit poetry of this kind relies upon the multiple meanings or coded associations of particular words, I have sometimes expanded in translation to suggest the erotic connotations of features such as scratches (acquired in foreplay) and reeds (cut down to make love), or to convey more than one meaning.

Bhāvakadevī

No. 646

At first, we were one thing –
Then you became my lover; I, suffering
The separation, your best beloved.
Now we are married: one man, one wife.
And what have I of life?
Only this fruit, cut for me by a bitter knife.

Vidyā

No. 807

Would you keep your eye, my neighbour, for a moment on my house?
He, the baby's father, won't drink the water from our well –
He finds it dull and tasteless. So I'd better go
Alone – would you mind the baby? – down to where
The river's stream is hidden by dense tamāla trees,
And the reeds, fresh cut, stand sharp and high.
Let them scratch me: you'll see, I'll come back torn,
On my back, my breasts, the soft part of my thigh.

No. 808

The very groves and vines drew round to watch
the gopīs take their pleasure, and the joy
of Rādha above all, upon the banks
of Jumna, Kalinda's princely son.

My friend, is it quiet there now? where once we cut
the foliage day by day to shape a bed
for memory and for love, there's not
any point now in such pruning care.

I know, you needn't tell me, how the buds
have flowered and fallen, the bright vines
hardened, spread, grown old, their bloom
rinsed off, like lips and fingers dulled by time.

Śīlabhattārikā

No. 815

The first man I lay with is my husband now
And this evening is just the same
As those nights when I felt filled
By moonlight, and the breeze came
Down from the Vindhya hills thick
With the scent of jasmine opening for the first time.

And I too am the same. So why
Does my heart so yearn again to lie
Behind a screen of reeds, in pleasure
So tender and so long to take
On the slope of the bank, on the rise of my waist.

GWERFUL MECHAIN

Translated by Zoë Brigley

Little is known about Gwerful Mechain, daughter of Hywel Fychan from Mechain in Powys. We only know Gwerful from her erotic, defiant poems and exchanges with male poets like Dafydd Llwyd and Dafydd ap Gwilym. Her poems often challenge the shame that women feel about their bodies even today: they are witty, celebratory, outrageous, bold, dynamic, bawdy, shameless, playful, funny, and irreverent. In 'Gwerful Watches Her Friend Take a Shit,' the disgusting seems sensual and imbued with magic and humour. Gwerful is also extremely skilled with Welsh-language forms. The formal artistry and proto-feminist content unite perfectly in 'Gwerful Curses a Man For Beating a Woman,' which may be one of the first instances of a Welsh poet writing about domestic violence.

Apart from the sensuality and humour, there are also poems that admit the precariousness of things like 'Gwerful Tells Dafydd Llwyd About the End of the World.' These Medieval poems resonate astonishingly well with the doubt of the twenty-first century. For Gwerful, in the absence of certainty, the ecstasies of the body are an answer.

Past translations of Mechain tend to be very strict in replicating the original rhyming and formal patterns of the englyn, but my priority is capturing the spirit of what is said, seen through a modern lens of #metoo, violence against women and less privileged groups, 'slut shaming', and feminism. Still, as much as possible, the englyn's rhymes or half-rhymes and cynghanedd-like chiming are employed.

Gwerful Curses a Man for Beating a Woman

Into your chest, a sharp stone slides – slanted
               down to split your sternum wide:
      kneecaps shatter as hands try
      to hold the spurting heart inside.

Gwerful Watches Her Friend Take a Shit

She squats to let the piss rip – chuting from
               the cauldron beneath her slip;
      three holes – one gurgling out shit,
      the other a rainbow arc between her hips.

Gwerful Wets Her Petticoat

In my camisole wet through – my chemise
               and my sweet, silk panties too,
      I'll never be dry again, unless it is true
      that good fucks pass by like rainclouds in June.

Gwerful Tells Dafydd Llwyd About the End of the World

Before the wars, we'll look up at the stars – more miracles
               happen on oceans than at altars,
      and though presidents do give orders,
      witches strip and dance on the shore.

Translated by Ainee Jeong

The kisaeng was a female courtesan class during dynastic Korea.
A kisaeng simultaneously belonged to the lowest caste and was trained
in the arts, whereas most low-caste women were not allowed this
education. A kisaeng could express her sexuality despite strict
Confucianist social ideals. However, this artistic and sexual 'agency'
operated within the nature of her work, as kisaeng were technically
government slaves. Though she had intimate interactions with the
elite, she was not granted social mobility. While kisaeng art was
enjoyed as entertainment in its day, it has not been preserved
with care.

Hwang Jini is an exception. Famous for her intellect and beauty
during her time, Hwang Jini and her work have persisted. She is
arguably the best-known kisaeng, living on through anecdotal
histories and film or television re-imaginings. As a result, Hwang Jini
has been celebrated as a kisaeng pop icon more than a significant
literary figure, although her sijo initially contributed to her longevity.

Sijo is a traditional Korean verse form totalling an average of
44–48 syllables (about 14–16 syllables per line) for three lines,
following the structure of theme, development, and a conclusion
usually containing a volta. The kisaeng often sung sijo with musical or
percussive accompaniment. My translations aim to keep the narrative
progression and do not exceed 48 syllables. I have translated each line
of the Korean into a non-rhyming couplet, resulting in a six-line poem
in the English, where Korean had three. In translating Hwang Jini's
sijo, I reject the kisaeng's supposed destiny of ephemerality in the
hopes of letting her sing again.

Transient

Mountains are still who they used to be,
but streams are never who they were.

Streams flow without rest night and day,
so how can they remain the same?

Distinguished men are like these streams –
they go and do not return.

Hindsight

Look what I have done,
not seeing how I would ache.

If I had told you to stay,
it would not have been this way.

But I had not known how much
I would long for who I let go.

Expectation

I divide a December night
into halves down its length.

One part I fold in pleats and plaits
to store under my spring quilt,

and unwind coil by coil
for whenever my love arrives.

Ongoing

I love like a jade mountain
whose blue brook is like your affection.

Does a jade mountain turn
while its brook ebbs with time?

Still, you can't disremember –
you'll spill tears as you move on.

Misled

When have I been unfaithful,
when have I ever deceived you?

And yet in the dead of night
when there's no chance that it is you,

falling leaves feign your footsteps,
and my heart is shaken.

HỒ XUÂN HƯƠNG

Translated by Natalie Linh Bolderston

Hồ Xuân Hương was a Vietnamese poet born in the late eighteenth century, surviving into the early nineteenth century. Little can be confirmed about her life, but there are many popular stories about her. One anecdote illustrates her sense of humour; upon falling over, it is said that she threw off her embarrassment, claiming: 'Dang tay với thử trời cao thấp; xoạc cẳng đo xem đất vắn dài.' In English: 'I stretch my arms to learn the height of the sky; I spread my legs to measure the earth.' This is an example of 'xuất khẩu thành thơ' – poetry composed spontaneously from speech.

Written against the backdrop of a society largely dominated by men, Hồ's work provides a defiantly honest and unsanitised female perspective. She offers bold portrayals of desire, women's bodies, power relations, and the stifling nature of tradition through deceptively basic images. Her poems seize on the latent power and beauty of everyday activities and objects – such as domestic chores and food – often imbuing these with subtle sensual undertones or more daring and humorous innuendo. In this way, Hồ builds a quiet but persistent sense of collective female insurgence and solidarity.

As a poet with Vietnamese heritage, I'm interested in the history of Vietnam as told by women; therefore, Hồ's close attention to women's spaces and inner lives drew me to her work. Fittingly, these English-language adaptations are the result of many conversations with my extraordinary mother, who provided the bridge translations and explained the idioms.

Notes: 'Xì xòm' are onomatopoeic words evoking the sound of water being bailed.
'Moon and wind' refers to a love affair.

To Bail Water

My sisters, when rain cracks the heat
let us bail water together.
Bring your three-cornered buckets on strings;
float with me on this four-shored rice field.
Xì xòm, we bend and straighten, heads thrown back,
swaying buttocks reflected in the rivers.
We work away our stiffness,
stand with our legs apart until the field is full.

New Year Couplet

On the thirtieth night, we seal the sky and soil against demons,
then unlatch the first morning, let every woman gather spring in her arms.

Sudden Pregnancy

I'm all awe and unfinished chemistry –
how much can my lover see?
God raises his head
to a willow girl with a spreading centre.
Did a century mean the same to my lover?
This heart is one of many I carry
as I close my eyes to the hundred-mouthed horizon
and know I am worth all that I hold.

To the Girl in the Painting

Sister, tell me the years
behind your beautiful face.
Know that young love is as pure as blank paper.
In a thousand years, you will still be the image of spring.
A fallen apricot dares not think of the moon and wind,
and the willow accepts her brittle fate.
Sister, why not draw from other pleasures?
I blame your painter, his apathetic skill.

Jackfruit

I swell like a late summer jackfruit.
My skin roughens, the pulp of my body so thick.
I wait to be speared and wanted.
If squeezed, I'll leave my colour on your hands.

Weaving at Night

The light reflects off every white surface
as we weave through the night.
Our feet push and lift,
and spools thrust to life.
Wide or narrow,
all fit our frames.
Sisters, hold down your fabric in water –
come autumn, it will find its true colour.

LOUISA SIEFERT

Translated by Katie Kirkpatrick

Siefert's writing carries within it a feeling of light: she conjures up the sun, the moon, the lights of the stage. I was drawn to this particular poem's strikingly modern voice and themes. 'After the Matinée' is a reflection of Siefert's own experiences with physical pain, but it can also be read as a discussion of a universal struggle.

Siefert's life was described by twentieth century French writer Lucien Scheler as 'a life illuminated by the beauty of the verb', and I think that rings true in this poem. Growing up in Lyon in the mid-nineteenth century, Siefert's adolescence was darkened by chronic illness. After turning to writing, her first collection, *Rayons Perdus* (1868) sold out, and her work was praised by Arthur Rimbaud and Victor Hugo. Siefert and her female peers contributed so much to French poetry, and yet remain largely forgotten.

Personally, I loved the idea of Siefert as a writer similar to myself but at a different point in time. She started writing poetry at the age of fifteen, and her best-selling book was released at twenty-three – an early incarnation of the modern day 'young poet'. Her themes are also similar to my own: she writes about personal nostalgia and memories. I hope I have done her justice in bringing her work back into the light.

After the Matinée

Well! I'm a triumph, the applause is deafening.
I knew how to laugh, to sing, to act out the play,
how to be young, once; to respond to each 'hello',
every 'how are you?' – another mundanity.
A lightning strike straight to the heart; a red rose against my cheek.

Well! It's true, I did it all, this is my confession.
But in spite of all that peace
(all still, all quiet, all satisfied, all happy)
and all the friends that surrounded me,
like the rising swell of the waiting tide,
I listened, I felt, at that same moment,
a never-ending rumble at the floodgates of my heart:
the deaf sea of my old tears.

One audience member knew, when, my hands in his,
he cast his gaze on me, dropped his anchor
and, with one quick glance, dived to the bottom.
Everyone else? No. Of all the anguish I've suffered,
they know nothing. I was always brilliant, always alive,
every time I walked away I came back with a wider smile.
When it was over, they all complimented me
on the exquisite naturalism and effortless panache
with which I acted out the play.

MÀIRI MHÒR NAN ÒRAN

Translated by Rosanna Hildyard

Many indigenous languages are spoken in the UK, including
Cornish, Welsh, Romani, Northumbrian. These are usually regional
and working-class languages: they belong to artisans and farmers;
particular skills, music, landscapes and stories. Marginalising
indigenous languages and multilinguilism in favour of English is not
just morally wrong; it's also silly, because English itself is an
intrinsically raggedy and various quilt of a language, pieced together
from scraps of Greek and Latin, Norse, Anglo-Saxon and French.
If any place can cope with a rainbow of tongues, it should be here.
Yet our indigenous languages have been systematically removed
from our culture, education and economy.

Màiri Mhòr nan Òran ('Big Mary of the Songs') was a nineteenth
century Gaelic-speaker who began composing poetry in her fifties,
when she was working as a servant in Inverness. She was accused of
theft and sentenced to forty days' imprisonment. She later said that it
was this humiliation within the English-skewed legal system that
set her writing.

Màiri Mhòr's songs deal with language and land; in particular,
the struggles of the (Gaelic) crofters who were thrown off their farms
in order for (English) landlords to profit. Though well-known in
Scotland, her work, as far as I can tell, has never been translated –
and indeed, Màiri Mhòr would surely not have wanted to be
translated into English. However, I hope my loose translation of one
of her songs will draw attention to her, to indigenous languages,
and hopefully act as an entry point into her work.

From *I'm Tired of the English*

I'm tired of their English language.
I'm tired of them and their fat tongue;
like that one pisshead guest who stays too long,
talking, till the sun's up and I'm tired, tired of them.

                                  ◆

Here, my words are the silver of scratchcards,
my voice a rattle of dice. Lucky to catch
the echo of a *sorry* as they push past – pitiless,
and my sentences shuffle, but I know I've no chance.

You know, where I was raised,
the earth itself would rise and back me.
No Saxon could shovel shit on me,
the soil itself would speak for me.

                                  ◆

My granny's a queen and you can't even
speak her name, it rips apart your tastebuds
bitter and warm as a cat's lick. And you, gagging
on it, when we got our name before your Jesus.

Sometimes I am too tired. Could fall
and lie facedown on my belly
with your meaty tread over my bones
and your weather filling my eyes.

New airs blow north, new graces. I hear
my own cadences soften and fall. New airs
stir the warmer waters, up north, my inflections.
Soft acid rain falls, the salmon blistering.

◆

Purple light I'm dancing in and for a flash
I think the singer's singing in my accent.
Is that how home used to sound: so
songlike? Oh, and the deer talked, too, I suppose?

The grass used to crawl with people,
the air filled with voices. Today,
the only person is the wrinkled forehead
of our crag, and sheep cropping graves.

◆

They are still lost, no matter the language.

'Finding the Right Pitch': An Appreciation of Lakshmi Holmström (1935–2016)

by Shash Trevett

Lakshmi Holmström (1935–2016) an Indian-born British writer and translator, came to translation late in life, after retiring from teaching English in India. Her first work to be published in the UK, *Inner Courtyard: Stories by Indian Women* (Virago, 1990), contained her translations of short stories from Urdu, Bengali, Kannada, Malayalam, Hindi and Tamil. It was the first anthology about the lives of women on the Subcontinent to be published by a major publishing house in the UK. Lakshmi became a prolific translator of Tamil prose and poetry, translating novels (by Ambai, Salma, Ashokamitran, Sundara Ramaswamy); collections of short stories (Pudumaippitan, Mauni, Ambai, Muthuswamy) and poetry from both India and Sri Lanka. She was instrumental in bringing the voices of Tamil women, especially, to readers in the West. Of particular note was her award-winning translation of Bama's *Karukku*, the first autobiography by a Dalit writer, which had faced hostility and rejection from the Tamil publishing industry in India. Lakshmi's vast output won her awards and recognition world-wide including the Iyal Award from the Tamil Literary Garden in Canada, and an MBE in 2011 for services to literature.

Tamil is one of longest surviving classical languages in the world dating back (in recorded form) more than 2000 years. Translating Tamil poetry or prose can be full of pitfalls and difficulties for the translator. Unlike English, it is a verb-final language, with a free word order within lines which always end with a finite verb. The elements of a sentence or a line – whether subject, object, adverb – can be placed anywhere, the subclauses arranged in order of time and sequence, which gives a sense of logic to the line. Sometimes, lines or

Shash Trevett by Lily Arnold

sentences can be subjectless – subject and object needing to be worked out from the linguistic context of the piece of writing – and are often constructed without use of punctuation. Moreover, Tamil is an agglutinative language, in which new words are formed (sometimes occupying entire lines) by the gluing on of other words. A translator has to unglue the joins, work out the tense and context by examining the use of suffixes, and convey the poet's intent with enough fluidity to capture the imagination of the anglophone reader. It is very difficult to achieve an iconic translation of a Tamil poem into English: it is almost impossible to match punctuation marks (where they exist), clauses or even line lengths. The only way a translator can negotiate between the two languages is by the skillful use of inversion, while still paying attention to the logic of time and sequence in the Tamil original. The beauty of Lakshmi's translations is that she seemed to overcome all these obstacles so effortlessly.

When the Tamil poets of Sri Lanka turned their pens to documenting the 30 years of wasted lives and memories from the civil war, they invented a new aesthetic of suffering. Lakshmi's translations, often in collaboration with Sascha Ebeling, were not just beautiful renderings of this poetry of trauma, they were almost historical documents, witness statements, of the atrocities being committed on the island. They brought to the Western reader news from the war zone. S Sivaramani (1968–1991) was a talented young poet from Jaffna, Sri Lanka, who committed suicide after burning her work. The poems we now have access to were either in the possession of her friends, or had been published in magazines. These were collated and published as *Sivaramani Kavithaikal* (1993) by the Women's Study Circle, Jaffna. Here is a verse from her poem 'Oppressed by Nights of War', in which she laments the loss of innocence in children traumatised by war.

நட்சத்திரம் நிறைந்த இரவில்

அதன் அமைதியை உடைத்து வெடித்த

ஒரு தனித்த துப்பாக்கிச் சன்னத்தின் ஓசை

எல்லாக் குழந்தைக் கதைகளினதும் அர்த்தத்தை

இல்லா தொழித்தது.

A literal translation of these lines would read thus (notice the finite verb at the end of the verse).

> In a star filled night
> its peace broken apart
> the sound of a lone gun
> the meaning of all children's stories
> destroys.

Here is Lakshmi's translation of this verse:

> Even the faint sound of a lone gun
> shatters the silence
> of a starry night
> destroying forever
> what children's stories tell.

You will notice the skillful use of inversion here. The gun becomes prominent, much like its prominence in the lives of these traumatised children; even the night bows down to it. Interestingly Lakshmi chooses to retain the verb at the end of the verse, rather than translating those lines as 'destroying forever | that told by children's stories.' Her version is elegant, and by retaining the verb at the end, she mirrors the syntax of the Tamil original, even as she changes emphasis from the gun to the stories. In her translation, she captures the essence of Sivaramani's powerful poem: that warfare not only destroys the innocence of children, it prevents an entire generation from believing in a world of make-believe, of magic and fairy tale, where the good overcome evil and the unworthy are punished.

Cheran is one of the best-known Tamil poets writing today. His renowned poem 'I Could Forget All This' (1983) is a long drawn out scream, written in a single sentence, about the brutal pogrom against the Tamils by the Sri Lankan state in 1983. Here is an excerpt from the middle of it:

எரிந்துகொண்டிருக்கும் வீட்டிலிருந்து
தொட்டில் ஒன்றைச்
சுமக்க முடியாமல் சுமந்துபோன
ஒரு சிங்களக் கர்ப்பிணிப் பெண்ணை [...]

The literal translations would read:

> from the house which is burning
> a cradle
> unable to carry yet carried away
> by a pregnant Sinhala woman

This has been lyrically translated by Lakshmi as:

> a Sinhala woman, pregnant,
> bearing, unbearably,
> a cradle from a burning house

Whether the occupant of the cradle was also left burning in that burning house is unclear. Lakshmi changes the repeated 'carry' of the Tamil original, to 'bear', thus adding another layer of meaning to the lines. It is almost unbearable for the reader to witness the single-minded purpose of the pregnant Sinhala woman intent on securing for her own, a future denied the Tamil occupant of that cradle. In Sri Lanka, where the Sinhalese don't read Tamil and the Tamils don't know Sinhala, these translations into English should have acted as a mirror, a point of reckoning. It should have been unbearable for the Sinhala nation to witness the spectacle of itself in these lines by Cheran. Yet 37 years after this poem was written, and given the current political climate on the Island, it would seem as if these words have failed to reach an audience that most needed to read them.

Lakshmi endeavoured in her translations to transmigrate centuries of history and culture from India and Sri Lanka to a new audience. Indian Tamil writers wrote about social or gender issues for a Tamil audience. Tamil poets from Sri Lanka were preoccupied with poetry as a means of gaining a voice when denied one by persecution. Yet when Lakshmi Holmstrom transplanted these magnificent Tamil writings to the West, she sought to make them universal; in this, she was exceptionally successful.

MARINA TSVETAEVA

Translated by Helen Mort

I have been fascinated by Marina Tsvetaeva's life and work since I discovered the dreamy films of Andrey Tarkovsky. I learned about the turbulent friendship between Tsvetaeva and Tarkovsky's poet father, Arseny Tarkovsky, tinged by unrequited love on her part. Tsvetaeva hanged herself on August 31, 1941 and Tarkovsky was hounded by guilt. What I find in Tsvetaeva's work is an intense, aching loneliness matched by searing intellect and wit. I have an almost physical reaction to her poems: they terrify me with their brilliance, the wistful quality that belies a deeper sense of isolation.

During the Covid-19 lockdown, I came across her poem 'I'd Like to Live with You' and it set me thinking about the challenges of either being marooned on your own or of being confined with a partner. The piece is playful, dark, describing a sleepy town, an ambivalent relationship. I began to 'triangulate' different versions of the poem, Google-Translating the original (helpfully, my stepson was in the midst of a university Russian exam at the time) and my own response emerged. I particularly wanted to bring out what I felt was an ambiguity in the poem around the words 'you would lie'. In some translations, this was interpreted as 'you would lie down', evoking an image of the lover, languid and sprawling. I wanted to preserve the other meaning of 'lie', the sense of deception and betrayal, picking up on an earlier phrase: 'and if you didn't love me, I wouldn't care'. Should we believe this? Tsvetaeva's work remains enigmatic.

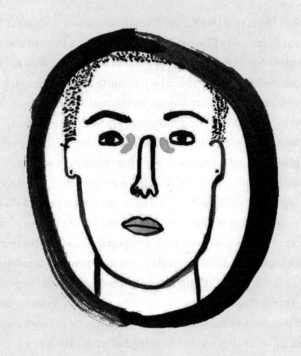

Helen Mort by Lily Arnold

I'd Like to Live With You

in a one-horse town
where it's always dusk
and bells don't stop chiming
and the pubs echo
with old clocks
time drizzling
and sometimes, at sundown, from an attic
a flute
and the player in the window
framed by big tulips
and if you didn't love me, I wouldn't care.

In the centre of our room – a huge tiled oven
each tile branded with an image
– rose – heart – ship –
and in the single window
snow three times.

You would lie – I love you
like this: idle, indifferent, carefree.
Now and then, the fizz
of a struck match,

the roll-up glowing down
to a tremble of ash
suspended
and you too lazy to even flick it
and everything always
on fire.

PARVIN ETESAMI

Translated by Nasim Rebecca Asl

Parvin Etesami (1907–1941) had a tragically short life. She was
something of a poetic prodigy – her first Diwan (collection) was
published when she was 28 and featured over 150 poems. She was
politically minded, and grew up attending literary meetings held by
her father and attended by some of Iran's most famous male writers.
Her death at age 34, from typhoid, was sudden and unexpected.
Parvin began writing her own poetry as a teenager and consistently
used classical Persian traditions in the style of her work. She was
instrumental in keeping nearly-forgotten forms alive and drew upon
nature, Aesop's fables and her own moral reasoning as inspiration.

Her poetry was noticeably modern. She was outspoken about the
oppression felt by women, not only in the Iran of the early twentieth
century, but throughout the nation's history. A forward thinker, she
was openly critical of the authoritarian policies enacted by leader of
Iran, Reza Shah, and reflections on the socio-economic implications
of his reign were present throughout her work.

Parvin's poetry has been taught in Iranian schools since her death;
my father can still recall verses he was taught to recite when in his
classrooms throughout the 1960s and 70s. Parvin was born in Tabriz,
a city in the north-west of Iran not too far from the area that has been
home to generations of my own family. She grew up in Tehran, like
my own father – he was the one that introduced me to her writing.

An SUV Drives Through the Capital

Blue lights guide a sea of traffic. Rusting cars lap
against the pavement. Cold hands wave
themselves warm, a patter of applause rolls with the convoy.
A thin girl taps her feet on her father's bony chest,
almond eyes squinting over the Friday crowd.
Baba, who is that? Why do they have such a fancy car?
Her new voice is lost in the fanfare of horns.
Baba, can we buy a car like that? A woman veiled

in exhaust fumes sputters to their left: *Oh baby*
things like that are not for people like us. The man hiding
in that truck is a baddy. He doesn't care about people
like us. That's how he's got so rich. Be careful, little one –
he may look like us and sound like us, but he is a Wolf
wrapped in our skin. He'd eat you all up if given the chance,
the liar and fool that he is. Her lip twitches.
His scars remind him no reply is safest so the father leaves, pushes

through bodies as though practising how he'll fight
for space in the back of the stranger's truck next spring; as he shakes
his head his daughter sways like she will sway next summer
in the orange boat that'll steal her brother. Her father rocks
and rocks. His hands anchor her to him. The woman watches
the family vanish. From her chestnut eyes drops a single tear.
The powerful feed on fear. The gathered people Telegram
silent curses to their neighbours.

Through tinted windows, the Wolf spots the girl
swimming above his subjects' heads. He forgets
her dusty face in seconds. His SUV drives on.

YOSANO AKIKO

Translated by Clara Marino and Yui Kajita

Yosano Akiko (1878–1942), née Hō Shō, is one of the leading figures of twentieth-century Japanese poetry. In her prolific career, she wrote more than 50,000 tanka, 600 modern poems, and numerous essays of social criticism. She is best known for her controversial and innovative poetry, in which she openly explores themes such as female sexuality and motherhood. In addition, her translation of *The Tale of Genji* into modern Japanese is valued as a definitive text.

Yosano began composing tanka when she was around twenty years old. Her early work was published in *Myōjō* (*Bright Star*), a Romanticist magazine established by her future husband, Yosano Tekkan. Her first collection of tanka, *Midaregami* (*Tangled Hair*), became notorious for her provocative, unflinching portrayal of romantic passion. Her call for women to express themselves as independent individuals also left a deep impression on readers, especially as it ran counter to strict mores of the time that forbid women from being self-reliant or assertive.

'Nezumi' ('Mice') appears in the *Yosano Akiko zenshū* (*Yosano Akiko Complete Collection*), which was first published in 1929 and gathers 421 modern poems that Yosano selected from her contributions to magazines and newspapers. Although Yosano is best known for her tanka, the *Complete Collection* demonstrates the range of her poetic voice and her command over various styles and registers. This work, however, has been largely overlooked in the West. By reviving and re-examining these poems, we can enrich our understanding of a true pioneer of modern Japanese literature.

Mice

Mice live in my ceiling,
and they squeak like
a sculptor chiselling a
statue all through the night.
And when they dance
with their sweethearts their
pirouettes echo with the
force of racing horses.
Above, as I write,
clouds of dust
float down the attic,
but somehow they
are unaware.
But still, I feel that
I live with those mice,
and hope they have ample food
and nice warm dens
and that from time to time they
open a hole in the ceiling
and look in on me.

SELMA MEERBAUM-EISINGER

Translated by Ella Duffy

Selma Meerbaum-Eisinger (1924–1942), a German-speaking Jewish poet, was 18 years old when she died in the Michailowka labour camp. Selma began writing and translating poetry aged 15. Her handwritten and handbound collection, *Blütenlese* (Harvest of Blossom), consisted of 57 poems and was preserved by her friends during and after the war.

I was first introduced to Selma's work by a German-speaking friend, who shared a few poems from *Blütenlese* with me. They had the simplicity and clarity of a glass of water, but beneath their meniscus was intense feeling. Full of longing and frustration, both personal and political, we view Selma's world through an ever-changing landscape of seasons, weather and colour. The natural world becomes a way of understanding the human.

The rain is particularly present in Selma's work. In this poem 'Rain', we see how her closeness to the natural world, the intense gathering of her senses to properly notice her surroundings, leads to a glimpse of her emotional state – as if the world were a mirror. We have no way of knowing how Selma's work might have progressed, but these luminous poems of her youth sound, to me, like the authentic note of a gifted lyric poet.

Rain

You leave. And the pavement is suddenly wet
and the trees are newly green
and there's the smell of harvested hay.
You are hot and pale and in need of rain.

The grasses, dusty and sick,
curled to meet the ground,
sit up when a swallow bows close.
But you walk on. Alone,
you don't know how to feel.

And here and there, a hint of sun,
as if the light had no care for rain.

MASCHA KALÉKO

Translated by Sue Vickerman

I first encountered this poem in Germany, on a hand-out for a church Advent service. An obsession with Christmas (the dark side) is to be found in my own poetry, and I uncovered that the 'December blues' was a bit of a theme for Mascha Kaléko too. Her poems turn up in Christmassy German coffee-table books – even recipe books – as well as in Christian contexts.

Mascha quickly became famous in her twenties for her witty, satirical verses in Berlin newspapers. Her subject matter came from living alongside working-class Berliners and fellow refugees in crowded, cramped inner-city tenements between the wars. What strikes me most about Kaléko's poems is how she got alongside ordinary people – even sometimes writing in dialect – making acute observations of domestic life in a way that feels completely contemporary. To prevent throwing readers into some past time, I felt the need to swap the Mona Lisa print (smirking off the wall at the sad single guy) for a Kylie Minogue poster.

Mascha's 1950s comeback in Germany was short-lived. She returned to Berlin for the first time in 1956, and in 1959 would have received the Fontane Prize but turned it down: it was going to be handed over by a former Nazi official. Mascha has recently undergone a further German revival, but why has only one single volume of her poems been translated into English (Andreas Nolte, 2010)? She was prolific! And brilliant! And funny!

Single Guy, Christmas Eve

No place could feel more empty than my flat
at this moment. As late-shift shop workers head home at last,
Christmas rains down its blows. I am attacked.

Happy families shite – I don't do that.
But singlehood has never felt so crap.
I pace my silent kitchen. Forward. Back.
On the fridge, Kylie. Who you laughing at?

Tick tock. On my desk, the clock of a saddo.
On-screen, church bells. Ding dong. 'Silent Night' sung solo.
They've thought of me back home and posted gifts,
the local factory's fancy biscuits,
tie as usual, and a scarf – one of my mother's home-knits.

So I've asked me over. Come to my place!
Departmental Team Leader. Of Division 6.
Bachelor pad, part-furnished. Face it:
I've missed my best chances in life's grand race.
Roads not taken. Boat to wedded bliss.

This yawning space. Outside, starting to sleet.
My Christmas tree looks at me, green and bare.
Forget the tinsel, let's get out of here,
slope off into white-smattered side-streets,
play at spying on strangers.
A lone man hovers at windows down bleak
forgotten alleyways, and stares...

Dusk damping down to dark, and still the sleet.
Sick-making sentiment is what I dread.
Time for a nice single malt. Hint of peat.

Down to the local – just pop my head in!
It's dead. I wave the barman a greeting:
G'night! Can't stop – stuff still to do. Nuff said.

S. CORINNA BILLE

Translated by Yvette Siegert

In 2014, I spent several weeks at Übersetzerhaus Looren, a translation residency outside Zürich, Switzerland. Each translator's bedroom was named after a national writer, and I was assigned to the S. Corinna Bille room. It was my first encounter with her name, which seemed to reverberate with several possibilities of pronunciation. Was it 'Bille' as in 'billiard ball', I wondered, or did it rhyme with *ville*? Was the liquid 'l' sound lost, as in *billet*? Or could that 'e' contribute a subtle final schwa?

Stéphanie Corinna Bille (1912–1979) was born in Lausanne, in the French-speaking part of Switzerland, but spent most of her life in the multilingual southwestern canton of Valais. This landscape, known for the Matterhorn and the rich, contrasting colours and climate of the Rhône Valley, is the setting for much of Bille's lyrical, multifaceted work. The elusive strangeness of her French prose poems kept me company as I translated a poet from another language and as my tongue tried to ease back into the cadences of German. Two years later, I moved to Geneva and resolved to get ahold of everything Bille had ever written: *Théoda*, her brilliant account of love and murder; the Gallimard edition of her sweet and baffling *Cents petites histoires d'amour*; and, especially, the bougainvillea-coloured volume of her *Cent petites histoires cruelles*, with its spare prelapsarian tales that flicker suddenly into grim, haunted parables. These are the poems that helped me settle in Switzerland, even as they continue to unsettle me.

From *One Hundred Short Tales of Cruelty*

6. Grapes

One day I went inside a chapel here in the Haut-Valais. It was so dark in there, and so cruel, I had to hold my heart in both my hands.

The vaults hung low, and the saints lay all bloodless in their glass coffins. I felt weak and had to sit down. There I fell asleep.

When I woke up, I saw that I was a prisoner. A grapevine, which entwined around the columns of the altar, had reached all the way down to me. Its tendrils cinched my waist, its greenish vines roped heavily around my head. I drew my parched lips to its frosted, cloudy clusters – their powdery film like crystal myrrh – and felt my teeth crunching into glass grapes.

8. Night

The house was plunged into darkness, and I was so frightened I started walking in the dark.

Suddenly I was hit by *somebody*. I flailed angrily, but my fists met nothing but air. I felt around but found nothing.

I was so frightened I just kept going. Again *somebody* hit me. So I clutched at the invisible, but my arms only clasped my own body. I heard laughter, and then some hair brushed up against me. Hair like silk twine, which – to my surprise – I could hold onto. 'I've got you this time!' I said.

With a steady hand, I felt along the strands all the way up to the roots. The hairline curved like a hill down to the brow. A brow? I felt for a face, a body.

Nothing but empty space.

9. The Mirror

When I wished to look in the mirror – it was pretty, with a polished silver frame – I could not see myself in it.

But I kept studying it. The old glass, a bit tarnished, reflected the objects behind me: a dresser with a pitcher, a pink carnation in a black bowl.

I'm dreaming, I thought, and pinched myself. Bruises formed on my arms and thighs. But the mirror refused me.

With a shaking hand, I examined it and turned it over, until I finally smashed it against a bronze door knocker.

But then I picked up one of the shards, and there, in this star I held between my fingers, I could see two tears: two crystal pendants.

10. My Hand

One day my hand stopped obeying me. It pulled away from me, then it hardened. I watched in horror as it grew: its fingers spread, it thickened and lengthened. Phalanges entangling with branches, a nail splitting apart. I could see the sun through it.

I thought of branches and foliage. But it had neither of these: it was naked and ashamed, it had a hole like a stigmata.

But suddenly (joy) there was a beautiful red woodpecker, escaping from it.

Translated by Alex Mepham

Here we resurrect Gunvor Hofmo (1921–1995), one of Norway's most significant post-war modernists. Hofmo's early adulthood was left scarred by the horrors of war. In 1942 Hofmo's good friend and Austrian-Jewish refugee, Ruth Maier, was arrested in Nazi-occupied Norway, deported and murdered in Auschwitz. This event led to Hofmo's hospitalisation for depression in 1943. Between 1946 and 1955, Hofmo published five collections of poetry, commenting upon the destruction of meaning and humanity in the Second World War. During this time, Hofmo lived with Astrid Tollefsen, another Norwegian poet, becoming one of few Norwegians to live in an openly lesbian relationship. Following the five collections, Hofmo was committed for sixteen years at Gaustad Hospital with paranoid schizophrenia, during which time she did not write. After her discharge, Hofmo published a further fifteen collections of poetry between 1971–1994, of a more stripped-back, meditative style. For the last eighteen years of her life, Hofmo never left her apartment in Nordstrand, Oslo.

Both 'God Doesn't Talk' and 'I Want to Lead the Army' were published after Hofmo's silent period, characterised by mature reflection as opposed to passionate outpourings of emotion. Still, existential angst, restitution and pain are considered in these poems with restrained descriptions, simple metaphors, and plain syntax. Through poetry Hofmo was able to resurrect in memoriam the life of Ruth Maier, and Homfo herself from her sixteen years of silence. Now, with the publication of these two translations, begins the resurrection of Hofmo to a wider audience and a new generation.

I Want to Lead The Army

I want to lead the army
of the dead
with my face
wet with night and
wind
we will come
to the murderers at
night
stand by their beds
watch them when they
sleep
with faces like
ours
when God drives us
on towards atonement.

God Doesn't Talk

God doesn't talk to
me like to Moses
doesn't strike me down
like Job
but He is in the
horrific silence
inside of me.
Slowly He unfolds
himself
like the first light green
leaves of the birch tree.

MIRI BEN SIMHON

Translated by Lisa Katz

I first translated Miri Ben Simhon in 1998, a poem about mother-daughter relations, at the request of the editors of *The Defiant Muse*, who were compiling the Feminist Press anthology of women's poetry in Hebrew. I couldn't consult with the poet, who had died two years earlier, run over by a truck in a rural area in what may have been a suicide. I find her work mysterious, yet there may be an advantage in translating unusual juxtapositions of images without knowing what is 'meant': a freshness and surprise to the result.

I returned to Ben Simhon's poetry about five years ago, after two decades of experience translating. Her poetry does not appear to have been edited much in her lifetime, or since. The conciseness inherent in the Hebrew language saves the poems from chaos, but English translations may appear sloppy. She uses line breaks but punctuation appears only sporadically. Running-on is part of her style and I'm not sure how much the translator should be an arbiter of change. Hebrew has a penchant for using two words when one is enough, which English often does not. I've allowed myself some shrinkage. I know I am therefore guilty of 'clarification', the first item on Antoine Berman's list of 'Twelve Deforming Tendencies of Translation'. Then again, the huge English lexicon changes everything anyway.

My goal is to give voice to a twentieth century poet who has remained unheard in English. I hope that what emerges is a specific woman's soul examining itself, her specific (Jewish-Moroccan) origins, her specific location in the last decades of the twentieth century (Israel-Palestine), as well as the shared aspects of our lives.

Friends from Good Homes

I don't behave properly
and grow worse over time.
It's a fact that my friends
refuse to rob trains with me.
I know it's true
that upbringing and morality and the like
strongly influence this curious idea,
the robbing of trains which proudly and calmly bear
tattered canvas sacks of many salaries
from mines of coal or gold...
'But Miri, there are no gold mines in Israel,'
a friend said to me, his amazement turning to concern
and then to a study of the hidden agendas
swarming the battlefield of my soul.
'Look,' I said. 'The chances of being caught are nil –
I've planned it down to the last detail.'
'But...'
'No buts, it's obvious,' I spat out.
'Snakes writhe against me
behind your polite and cultivated mask, snakes...'
'That's enough,' my friend shouted
as everything clicked horribly inside his head.
'Look,' he said. 'First trains and now snakes.'
The phallic images clearly drove him crazy;
I don't speak properly.
Precise and polished mental plans for a robbery
make a person impossible to bear.
Truly it's no wonder that my friends refuse to rob trains,
but no surprise that I would consider it.

What do snakes have to do with this
except a clumsy, tail-like guilt?
There's no knowing my friends' sly intentions,
this renunciation of wealth (as real as the sun)
makes me suspicious right away –
of insults to my character I mean.
My friends refuse to rob snakes... that is, trains.
May God protect me from my friends,
there's something questionable about friendship.

NADĚŽDA PLÍŠKOVÁ

Translated by Ryan Scott

Known principally as a graphic artist, Naděžda Plíšková (1934–1999) wrote poems that detailed her marriage, motherhood, artistic milieu and life under communism in Czechoslovakia. Her unadorned language is a rare, albeit complicated, perspective of a woman poet from within a regime that did not recognise feminism and from within the mostly male dominated anti-establishment underground.

Though the communist period largely saw Plíšková focus on visual art, her poetry was occasionally published in *samizdat* (illegal publishing in the communist era) and received praise for its 'stripped down' quality. Her first official collections appeared after the Velvet Revolution. *The ABCs of Plíšková* (1991) blended her spare, and at times coarse, language with pictures and graphics. *Pub Romance* (1998) was based on conversations overheard in her favourite haunts. She lent this setting, more often associated with male writers, humour and humanity, treating it with an amused detachment. Her final collection *Plíšková for herself* was released a year after her death. The personal subject matter of these poems resonates not simply because of the unvarnished depiction but because Plíšková's treats it, as one critic said, with self-reflection and self-irony.

'Verse I Found in a Trunk', from the last book, deals explicitly with the neglect she suffered from her husband Karel Nepraš. But it is more than a plea for affection. Adjusting and readjusting the emphasis of her words, Plíšková simulates a struggle to communicate some long-term partners' experience and in so doing expresses a more important need – the need to be heard.

Verse I Found in a Trunk

Karel
you haven't
Karel
touched me for years now
and you've said nothing kind
FOR YEARS NOW KAREL
you haven't touched me
and
you've said nothing kind
Karel
you haven't touched me
for years now
Karel
and you've said nothing kind now
for years Karel
you haven't touched me
and
you've said nothing kind
Karel
you haven't touched me
for years now
and
— — — — — — — —
— — —

NOÉMIA DE SOUSA

Translated by Belinda Zhawi

When approached to work on this project, I saw it as an opportunity to delve deeper into the works of African women poets who are no longer living, which was incredibly exciting. At first, I was interested in exploring the works of the Sierra Leonean poet, Gladys Casely-Hayford, because she was formidable and her work is easier to access in comparison to other African women poets. However, I started to think more deeply about the success of the divide-and-conquer project that was colonialism, and felt that old chasm between Anglophone, Francophone and Lusophone African writers. I decided to focus on Noémia de Sousa because I wanted to learn more about her work and other Lusophone poetry. Even though I do not speak Portuguese, I knew I would be able to understand and relate to the culture she is writing about.

Noémia de Sousa (1926–2002) was born in Catembe, Mozambique and is considered one of the leading African poets. Her oeuvre denounced Portuguese colonialism and built morale among FRELIMO, the guerilla soldiers fighting for Mozambican independence. Despite being widely read across Lusophone Africa since the late 40s, de Sousa's poems were only compiled and published in 2001 as *Sangue Negro*. 'Magaiça' is a poem about a 'mamparra' (simpleton) who migrates to South Africa for a 'better life', working in the mines, and later comes back home a shell of himself. Magaiça is a Mozambican Portuguese word used to describe individuals who left home to work in South African gold mines. This is the kind of story I grew up with as a young girl: the legend of Johannesburg. The men went there and never came back – and when they did, they returned mere shells of themselves. My Zimbabwean grandfather was a magaiça in 1950s South Africa. After he left, nobody saw or heard from him for more than a decade before he eventually made his way home. I have become such a migrant, who occasionally returns home with only fragments of their language and traditions. I read the poem in Portuguese and English then translated the English versions to Shona (my first language) then back into English.

Magaiça

The blue and gold morning of tourist brochures
overwhelmed the mamparra.
Dizzy at the incomprehensible hubbub
of Caucasian voices at the station
and the quavering breath of the trains
his eyes rounded in amazement,
his heart pressed with the anguish of the unknown,
his bundle of rags bearing the anxiety woven
    in the wished-for dreams of the mamparra.

Then, one day,
the train came back gasping, gasping...
oh, yes, it came back!
And with it, the migrant
in an overcoat, a scarf and striped socks,
an alien dressed in ridiculousness.

You carry your suitcases on your back
        – where did you leave your bundle of dreams, migrant? –
full of the false glow
of what's left of Rand's

false civilisation.
Stunned,
the migrant lights a hurricane lamp
and mines his palms
for lost illusions; for his youth
and health, buried
back in the mines of Jo'burg...
Youth and health,
the lost illusions
sparkle like stars in the low neckline
of any Lady
in the staggering lights of any City.

SHEILA CUSSONS

Translated by Andrew van der Vlies

Sheila Cussons was an artist and poet. Born and educated in South
Africa, she lived in Amsterdam and – with her Catalan husband and
two sons – in Barcelona, before returning to South Africa in 1983. She
died in Cape Town in 2004.

I first encountered her poetry at school in Port Elizabeth in the
early 1990s. Her collections had fabulously weird titles – *Die woedende
brood* (The Angry Bread); *Omtoorvuur* (Magically Transformative
Fire) – and something about her life resonated with my own sense (as
a queer adolescent) of being at odds with my surroundings. Despite
winning numerous prizes, including the prestigious Hertzogprys,
Cussons seemed out of synch with the main currents of Afrikaner
culture. Her Catholicism was unusual in a largely Calvinist milieu.
Nor did she appear to conform to apartheid's expectations of
'woman': she left her family in Spain, and with her face badly burned
in a domestic fire, didn't look (to me) like the photos of other female
poets in our textbooks (whether pious grandmother-cum-librarian
Elisabeth Eybers, or precocious rebel-cum-farmgirl Antjie Krog).
And then there was the poetry itself, balancing close observation of
the everyday – shot through with mysticism – with confessional
treatment of anxiety, in language that seemed gemlike one minute,
colloquial and comical the next. Cussons is Elizabeth Bishop *and*
Sylvia Plath, with flashes of John Donne and a twist of William
Carlos Williams, in Afrikaans. These are my *versions* of Cussons's
poems, respecting as closely as possible the effects of her metaphors
and (I hope) her humour.

Exile II

The neighbours' gibber outside swirls aloud.
I feel as far from self as a sore fish
on a baking deck, or hidden in mud,
which is the same.
I tiptoe through myself; nothing here is mine.
Up the stairs it beats oppressively,
and here below the air from summer-doors
can't help me.
My book has come. I stare at the letters, stumped,
estranged so from myself I cannot see
in the name on the cover me,
seven odd letters that spell 'Cussons' –
Between the chill indoors and heat outside, I sit
and page *sans* sense, search for my own point, but
find only vowels and complementary consonants.
I did want to clone myself, not so?
Now I try to slide from the deck, the mud,
into the waves once more. Page... tomorrow will come.
I've only to endure 'til then, have only to endure.

Supermarket

No longer do you only get what you receive,
can choose at will or whim: it's super(s)mart!
There are baskets and great trolleys
and rows of *proviand*
and you, glass-eyed, salivate: the choice!
with one at your side like another commission.
The cashier seems familiar too: she tallies
up the total quick. Gee whizz.
You lie your way out of it, lift your chin
against the sense of weight, from an under
and under the under an under – Nonsense:
your car waits high and cool.
But if, empty, you were to reach a hand to give,
and eyes surprised look up, fingers eagerly grasp,
a whole face like light, would you not kneel?
That's to say, *if* this were to happen?

Smoke Blooms: 'Resurrecting' Nadia Anjuman, January 2020

by Suzannah Evans

When Dead [Women] Poets Society invited me to resurrect a poet for their 2020 series of readings, I assumed (rightly or wrongly) that the poets who sprang easily to mind (U A Fanthorpe, Bishop, Plath, Audre Lorde) might well have been covered already and so I took it as an opportunity to discover a poet I had not yet heard of. I was also interested in finding poetry in translation; as a white anglophone poet who has always lived in the UK I'm keen to find countries, languages, experiences other than my own through my reading. I liked the idea that D[W]PS use at their 'séances' of entering into a conversation with women poets from the past, and bringing their work into the present, and I see translation as an extension of this conversation; an opening up of boundaries both international and ethereal.

It is not until I discovered Nadia Anjuman that these pieces started to fit together. I found her by accident, by Googling 'woman poet Afghanistan' or something similar following a conversation I had all but lost the thread of and wanted to retrace. It was a serendipitous mistake. I found a webpage with a stunning set of translations at brooklynrail.org by Diana Arterian and Marina Omar. I was so struck by these poems; their strong outlines, their beauty and natural imagery, their brutality, their understanding of grief and loss: 'I am closing the door on grief, becoming moonlight from head to toe' ('I Wish').

The short biography of Anjuman provided introduced me to the 'Golden Needle', an idea I loved; that Nadia as a teenager, along with other poets and literary scholars in her generation, had met at a nearby professor's house to study poetry, under the guise of working on their sewing skills. At this time, Herat was under Taliban rule, and

Suzannah Evans by Lily Arnold

education for women was not permitted unless it related to domestic duties. The professor's wife stayed nearby to assume the role of 'teacher' should anyone knock on the door, and under the fabric in the students' sewing bags were hidden books of poetry, pens and notebooks. I was enchanted by the idea of poetry as a quiet resistance; that even carrying a line of it with us in our heads is an act of defiance, if that is what is forbidden. I saw here something I have often thought about; that poetry and the act of writing can remind us of our humanity, help us maintain the hope we need to keep going, giving us a little bit of power in situations where we are powerless.

Anjuman was a master of the ghazal, a form with ancient Arabic origins, described by Mona Arshi as 'long trembling lines' that can 'bear holding [the] lyric music' (*How To be a Poet,* Nine Arches Press, 2018) and there is something about her poems that does tremble and shimmer, that at times manages to hold a great weight of emotion without crumbling. As part of reading and thinking about Anjuman I tried writing my own ghazals to see what those lines were capable of. I thought that as someone who is unable to read Persian/Dari this might at least give me a slight feeling for the process of her writing. I found that the lines of these poems can feel like branches or long roots, and where they take us can be surprising; places where beautiful imagery and powerful ideas can be brought into balance. Ghazals traditionally include a repeated word at the end of each couplet; reaching that word as a writer and a reader feels like landing on solid, familiar ground each time.

Once Herat was free of the Taliban, Nadia was able to officially enrol at the university to study literature and write poetry, and join the local literary society, Anjuman-e-Adabi, the group she took her pen name from, which I think speaks of the value she placed on literary community. She was the first woman poet to publish a book in Herat after the Taliban, in 2005. The book is *Gul-e-dodi,* which translates as *Smoke Bloom* or *Smoke Flower*. The title poem of this book holds at its centre the image of a flower being obscured and smothered by smoke: 'streaks of smoke begin | to obscure her face and fumes | consume her perfect skin' ('Smoke-bloom' in *Load Poems Like Guns*). Nadia's friend Gulsoom Sediqi, interviewed in Farzana Marie's *Load Poems Like Guns: Women's Poetry from Herat* (Holy Cow! Press, 2015) says that 'the metaphor in Nadia's poem is a heartbreakingly apt depiction of her own life'.

Nadia Anjuman had avoided marriage, describing herself as a scholar wanting to focus on her art, but married Majid Niā because he threatened suicide if she did not, manipulating her compassionate nature. He too was a scholar, and one very jealous of the success and attention Nadia was receiving. The same year her first book was published, 2005, he became violent during an argument and Nadia subsequently died from the injuries she received. The city's literary world erupted with outpourings of grief and poems in memory of her talent.

In resurrecting Nadia Anjuman, then, I was always going to have to tell the story of her tragic death, however much spotlight I wanted to give to the poems themselves. I remember as an undergraduate student noticing how many books about Sylvia Plath's life there were in the university library; many more than there were books she had written. I imagined those books of biography and speculation to be particularly frustrating for a poet, someone who was so skilled at defining the world in their own words. The last thing I wanted to do was to romanticise the untimely loss of a young poet; Anjuman's death is a call to raise domestic violence awareness and to fund services worldwide, but there is nothing inherently *poetic* about its tragedy.

There is so much about Anjuman's ambition, quiet revolution, her love of literary community, and of course the work itself, which inspires and resonates with me. However, I'm lucky enough that I've never had to study in secret under the threat of death or incarceration, and I was keen not to try to speak *for* her at any point. I was also worried about the idea of 'resurrecting' a poet from a culture that doesn't think about ghosts in the same way that I do. Although many Islamic cultures refer to Jinn, my understanding is that these are spirits who have always been spirits, and the dead rarely, if ever, appear to the living. However, even if Anjuman cannot appear as a spirit in the sense I use the word, I think she can be a presiding influence, remaining in conversation with us through the poems she wrote.

Further reading: poetry by Nadia Anjuman at brooklynrail.org:

intranslation.brooklynrail.org/persian-dari/poetry-by-nadia-anjuman

CHRISTA REINIG

Translated by Jenny O'Sullivan

Christa Reinig (1926–2008) was a feminist, lesbian poet and author.
Born to a cleaning woman during the Weimar Republic and clearing
away the debris of the Second World War as a teenage 'Trümmerfrau',
Reinig began her writing career in East Berlin, where she was later
banned from publication in the GDR.

I came upon Reinig after recognising that, after a four-year
German Literature degree, I could not confidently name a German
lesbian poet. Written after becoming severely disabled in the early
seventies, her 1979 work *Müßiggang ist aller Liebe Anfang* consists of a
short stanza for every day of the year, documenting a middle-aged
lesbian relationship through love, illness and mundanity.

I selected an extract from the opening and then one from August
to reflect the time of year when I was translating. Meandering
between tender, existential musings and bluntly comic asides, I love
how Reinig draws out details that feel timeless but somehow
overlooked, from the subtle feminist defiance in an act of DIY to the
potential sensuality of having nits. Her casually inconsistent diary
style presents straight forward language pepped with puns, which
made translation quite a deceptive challenge. Realising I could
translate 'Brotzeitalter' (a pun eliding 'Bronze Age' with an afternoon
break for bread-based snacks) as 'scone-age' was definitely a
highlight! But I've really enjoyed the closeness to her work that
translating permitted: this seventies story of middle-aged lesbian
mundanity offers me a window into a queer future and evidence
of a queer past.

From *Love Makes Work for Idle Hands*

January

9 Monday
   another body
   dying next to me
   what do I know

10 Tuesday
   don't leave me, swear you won't!
   I swear: if I ever
   have to leave you
   I'll take you with me

11 Wednesday
   the missus is ill, I say
   deary me! says the neighbour
   (thinks I mean housekeeper)

12 Thursday
   you can't die
   impossible
   to accept
   but I force myself

13 Friday
   tapping on the windowsill
   tears me from my bed
   the rain patters
   I dreamt you were crying

14 Saturday
   down how many hot coal paths
   have I defied the force of gravity
   simply: step by step
   did you know that

15 Sunday
    sat against the light
    the heavens shine through you
    through your eyes
    beaming towards me

16 Monday
    my thirsting fingers
    bathe in your hair
    drawing undue partings
    as if you had nits

August

24 Thursday
    our bamboo palace
    is your handywork
    woman-made
    I'm proud of that

25 Friday
    being so near to you
    that your two eyes
    become
    one big eye

26 Saturday
    maniac three sheets to the wind
    sails a zigzag course kidward
    M-CX 581 Audi 100 s
    burnt orange

27 Sunday
   tender vitality
   that I hold in my
   arms – long after
   it is gone

28 Monday
   if you were a flower
   I would flatten you
   in the telephone book

29 Tuesday
   after years of grievance we
   are now in the scone-
   age

30 Wednesday
   right at this moment
   there's a woman sitting somewhere
   thinking up things
   we can use

31 Thursday
   today once again
   I avoided a man
   on the stairs
   – automatically –

HELGA M. NOVAK

Translated by Karen Leeder

Helga M. Novak (1935–2013) was a German-Icelandic writer, who
lived an itinerant, anarchic and slightly mysterious life. Born in
Berlin, she spent the first five years in a children's home after her
father committed suicide. After leaving what she called 'an
unsuitable adoptive family' (Nazi supporters) she grew up in the
eastern zone of Germany, studying journalism and philosophy at
the University of Leipzig and also, as she later confessed, acting
as an informant for the East German secret police, but always
had a complicated relationship with authorities and any notion
of belonging.

After her GDR citizenship was revoked for publishing critical
texts, she moved to Iceland (taking her Icelandic name Maria
Karlsdottir), and travelled between West Germany, Bulgaria,
Portugal and Poland, always confrontational and rebellious, earning
her living salting fish in a factory or writing plays. When in 2004,
after living most of her life in exile, she tried to return to Germany,
'the greatest living German poet' (Wolf Biermann) was refused
citizenship.

Novak's early poetry embraced traditional forms, from ballads
to fragmentary sonnets and rhyme. With time came an increasing
stringency and anger. Immersed in the natural world, the poems,
like this one, also speak of an existential and poetic placelessness.
Her later poems are at once wounded and adamant – quite unlike
anything else. I have known her work for many years, though was
inspired to read her again when I translated a poem by Ulrike Almut
Sandig dedicated to her for MPT. She deserves to be known in
English.

Ach, I Stood at the Spring

Ach, I stood at the spring
arrived at last
I forgot to drink
surrounded by twigs
under a snowberry roof
I sat in the damp
hollow of stone
why
did I insist on going it alone
you had said –
I'll come with you to the spring

brooding in the cold
of water and moss
I sense
beneath the brightness of a sunny day
death all around
and think – it is all over
and I am rid of you

after I was out of that hell
I sank into a fox hole
that could not be seen
under the thorny scrub
ach I stood at the spring
and did not drink

GISÈLE PRASSINOS

Translated by Jade Cuttle

Gisèle Prassinos (1920–2015) was a French-speaking poet of Greek and Turkish heritage, largely erased from the narrative of twentieth century literary movements, despite being celebrated at the time by André Breton. Breton discovered her writing in 1934 when, at just fourteen, she was published in the French surrealist magazine *Minotaure* and the Belgian periodical *Documents 34*. Her first book, *La Sauterelle arthritique* (*The Arthritic Grasshopper*) was published in 1935 with a preface by Paul Éluard and a photograph by Man Ray.

The surreal nature of her writing flirts with multiple possibilities, promoting the vision that poetry can be viewed as a portal to parallel worlds. This idea repeatedly surfaces through the dream-like mist that lingers over the text, shifting logic where it pleases. The poet also has a sense of humour which comes to surface in unexpected and stimulating places, as is the nature of surrealist poetry. She had an intriguing, sometimes rebellious, questioning relationship with her mixed heritage background, which I find fascinating given my own reluctance to conform to reductive assumptions around identity. For this reason, I was pleased to resurrect Prassinos in February by writing and performing a song inspired by her work at a Dead [Women] Poets Society 'séance' at The Forum, Norwich. I continue to enjoy bringing attention to this thought-provoking poet.

Jade Cuttle by Lily Arnold

The Roof of My House

The roof of my house
rests on beams.
I don't know how to conform to their straightness.
I have to roam
always reaching beyond the illusion.

In the shaft of the main column
I see myself and straighten up.
If I can't, the column sorts me out.
Do not knock my dreams
fragile like an eye.

FADWA SULEIMAN

Translated by Marilyn Hacker

Fadwa Suleiman was born in Aleppo in 1970. Educated at the Higher
Institute for Dramatic Arts in Damascus, she was a well-known actor
in theatre, film and television until she joined the uprising for
citizens' rights and regime change in 2011. As a public figure, a
member of an Alawite family, and a moving speaker for the
revolution, she quickly became well known, too well known to remain
in Syria. She came to France as a political refugee in 2012.

Sometime in 2013, a friend sent round an email saying that Fadwa
Suleiman was seeking pupils for Arabic tutoring. 'Would you like to
take riding lessons from Joan of Arc?' was what the message seemed
like to me. Yes, I would! Fadwa, whom I had only seen in YouTube
videos addressing crowds of protesters in Homs, or leading
supporters of the Syrian revolution in chants on the Place du
Châtelet, arrived at my door a day not long afterwards, following a
brief telephone exchange, took off her shoes and came in. I made
coffee, and explained in halting Arabic that what I'd really like to
do was learn poems by heart – the way she had written that she had
done in drama school in Damascus. For the next couple of months,
she and I would sit at my upstairs wooden table with a volume of
(most often) Mahmoud Darwish's poems, and the paper on which I'd
copied them, to help in learning. And in between, and afterwards in a
café, we talked. One day, Fadwa said she 'couldn't take money from a
friend' for lessons – and I would not have her work for nothing. But
our friendship continued, and I began to translate some of her own
poems, in her first collection, كلّما بلغ القمر (As The Moon Rose).
Three years later, Fadwa was diagnosed with lung cancer; she died in
France in 2017.

Why?

Why are the people there naked?
We were smothered in polyester.

Why are there rows of tents there?
We were drowned in a clamor of metal.

Why was a people exiled?
They were drowned in a sea of blood.

And what is that deafening noise?
The suicide of alphabets
And time flooding into time.

What is that silence?
Cities dying, crushing their histories.

What is that cry?
My blood drowned in sand
My sun setting.

Ankita Saxena by Lily Arnold

FAHMIDA RIAZ

Translated by Ankita Saxena

Loud, ugly, unashamed and sometimes disrespectful, laughter can be an unexpected form of liberation. We rarely laugh in rooms that do not make us feel welcome. To laugh with someone, truly and not consciously, is to think yourself their equal. In 'Ek Aurat ki Hansi', Pakistani poet Fahmida Riaz portrays a woman's laughter as a sign of her 'azadi' (freedom). Like many of our foremothers, Riaz fought for her right to laugh – to laugh at the religious separatism in post-partition India and Pakistan (which she captures in her poem 'Tum Bilkul Hum Jaise Nikle') and at the continued suppression of marginalised voices.

Riaz also spent a lot of time honouring her lineage, working on translations of the female Farsi poet Forough Farrokhzad, as well as Rumi, into Urdu. Despite her often radical gaze, when Riaz passed away in 2018, she was celebrated on both sides of the border as an extraordinary voice of authority. In an interview, Riaz said: 'I am not an exceptionally politically over-charged poet. Perhaps the only exception is that I am a woman.'

I have grown up with women who laugh. My mother, who starts laughing midway through a story she is trying to tell you. My beautiful best friend, whose laugh emerges first in her eyes, then in the 'lush tremor' of her open mouth, before erupting finally into full-blown ecstasy. My translation is for all the women in my life, who have given, and continue to give me, me the permission to laugh.

A Woman is Laughing

Under the singing watch
of a rocky mountain
a woman is laughing.
No fame, no money
but bold with the guts
of a free body:
a woman laughing.

In all the world's temples,
you will not hear the lush tremor
of a woman laughing.
In the market of all treasures,
you will not find the baby balm
of a woman laughing.
This rare narcotic she bears
so freely cannot be captive, sold.

Come then, become breeze.
In the wild valley, lapping
her face with kisses –
hair flying long and loose,
wind's daughter is singing
alongside the wind:
a woman is laughing.

Let's Never Get Too Comfortable!

Katrina Naomi reviews *Songs We Learn From Trees: An Anthology of Ethiopian Amharic Poetry*, edited and translated by Chris Beckett and Alemu Tebeje, Carcanet, 2020

Chris Beckett and Alemu Tebeje's anthology of Ethiopian Amharic poetry is wonderful, not only for the choice of poems, but for the fluency and energy of the translations. The editors are also to be congratulated for their cogent introduction and the context they give to Ethiopian poetry.

First, a word on Amharic. While there are over 80 languages in Ethiopia, Amharic is used by poets from other linguistic and ethnic groups to reach a wider audience. Beckett and Tebeje set out the two main types of Amharic poetry: get'em and q'ine. 'Get'em' means rhyme and relies on a syllabic count. There is an ease of rhyming in Amharic compared to English. Q'ine poems have a religious theme. Q'ine poets strive for both a surface and a hidden meaning, known as semenna worq (wax and gold), which can give a critical, funny or even sexual subtext to a poem. This wax and gold sensibility is important, particularly in contemporary poetry of protest. As the editors state, 'you cannot always say what you think in Ethiopia without being locked up'.

Poetry only switched from being an oral form after Ethiopia's liberation from the Italian occupation in 1941. Under Haile Selassie, schools and universities were opened and some poets studied abroad, taking on poetic influences from elsewhere. After the fall of Selassie and rise of the Derg military junta in 1974, there was a brutal crackdown.

'Headache' is an anonymous get'em love poem, with a startling, and pleasing, frankness, which typifies many of this anthology's poems:

If I get a headache, I have myself bled.
If I get colic, I reach for a pill.
If I get VD, I jump in a spring.
But what can I do if he doesn't love me?

Writing in the twentieth century, the poet Gemoraw (Hailu Gebre-Yohannes)'s work feels highly contemporary in its critique of the (mis)use of innovations and technologies. He is just one of many poets to have been imprisoned by the authorities. Is it any wonder that protest poems are such a force in Ethiopia? The oral tradition is very much present in the anthology, as in his poem 'The gift of a curse':

You who invented the AEROPLANE, you *Wrong* Brothers!
was your aim to export a rubbish culture to the world?
to transport useless products and all sorts of things that
no-one needs from Yankiland?
Please fly to hell, Wrong Brothers, in your AEROPLANE!

Still in the vein of protest, Mengistu Lemma, who studied at the London School of Economics, writes poignantly of the racism he experienced in mid twentieth-century London. 'Longing' is set on a train:

The carriage was big enough for ten,
but no-one was brave enough to open the door
I'd shut fast to keep in the warmth.
Instead, they huddled in the corridor,
unwilling to share the warmth with a black man –
even though coal is black, even though
the wealth of England was forged by black coal.

Male poets dominate but the editors' efforts to ensure greater gender parity in the later sections of the anthology has brought protest poems from a women's perspective to the fore – including Misrak Terefe, whose unforgettable child-rape poem 'What did you find so beautiful' was included in *Modern Poetry in Translation* vol. 1, 2020. Meron Getnet's feminist and humorous poem, 'Prototype', riffs on the creation of men and women, with God having: 'sketched you first, | before He dreamed me into being | as the finished product'.

As well as protest, and love, poetry as fable is a strong theme. Mekdes Jemberu's contemporary poem 'Hypocrites' is an example:

> When a plough pulled by an ox
>   under its heavy yoke
> stumbles on a lump of earth
>   that will not break,
> the farmer always blames the ox,
>   never the earth,
> calls it a lazy beast and gives it
>   a good crack of his whip.

Jemberu founded the Ethiopian Women Writers Association and her work is much loved in Ethiopia.

One of the youngest poets featured, and one of my favourites, is Liyou Libsekal (b. 1990) who won the UK's 2014 Brunel University African Poetry Prize. Her writing blends tradition with a looser, possibly more personal style. I love her closing lines, including 'I am fragile in this disorder', from the poem 'Gospels' and 'falling as we must', from 'Into the Earth'. In the short poem 'Bearing Heavy Things' quoted in full here, much is left unsaid.

Living in the traditions of our men you unfolded young, and mothers and aunties whispered over scalding coffee and joyous incense.

They slaughtered a sheep for you, a day of melodic tongues, of wealth for your father and promise for his.

Pinned up over early bed you nursed on stray beams until you were left with brimming womb on fickle hips.

Now they shame you for your smell, for what your body lost when it couldn't hold; and yet again, you are ushered out of home.

Having been to Ethiopia, I know how insulting the West's singular focus on famine and drought has been (when Ethiopia is discussed at all). There are many strong poems inspired by hunger though. Nebiy Mekonnen was imprisoned and tortured for eight years in the 1970s–80s. His poem 'Servant of the Cloud' achieves that rare thing – something beautiful out of devastation, depicting a poor farmer:

> all he sees is this dry red morning sky
> a world without one drop of water
> a sky without an eye for ploughing...
> > now everyone is servant
> > or attendant of the cloud

It's possible some poems may seem slightly too moralistic or paternalistic to Western tastes, but the vast majority are a surprise and a joy. I'd like to end with a poem exemplifying the anthology's humour and subversion, with four lines from Alemayehu Gebrehiwot's 'OK, Let's Be Exiled', yet another great performance piece:

Let's go! let's rush
yes, let's be exiled,
[...]
Yes, let's return!
Let's never get too comfortable!

Some New Fixture in the Sky

Stephanie Sy-Quia reviews *After Callimachus* by Stephanie Burt, Princeton University Press, 2020

'If this book is a work of translation (and I hope it is!)', writes Stephanie Burt in the 'Imitator's Note' to her collection *After Callimachus*, 'it's also science fiction, or alternate history.' Her fifth collection of poetry, *After Callimachus* takes the work of the third century BCE poet, native to the Libyan city of Cyrene and thereafter resident of Alexandria, Egypt, as a series of footholds for transliterative flights of fancy. 'My goal,' Burt continues,

> has been, not a historically and linguistically precise reconstruction of his poems in their original Alexandrian and Hellenistic contexts, but rather a new Callimachus in contemporary English, a poet who feels at once close to the Greek original and like a fresh, coherent, wise, entertaining, and sometimes even humorous poet writing in mostly American English for readers today.

The resultant poems are peppered with playful anachronisms (nail polish, Taylor Swift) and semi-contemporary slang ('emo'). In Lyric, frag. 22, 'Aphrodite' is made to rhyme with 'karaoke' and 'panettone'. Athena meets Apollo for lunch in 'her peacetime daytime dress,' at 'the sunlit outdoor centre-city workplace, | the one with the gold columns'. Artemis goes to pick out puppies ('(yes, of course you get puppies)'), and they are 'black and half white, | like cookies', and 'one | with almond patches and alert black ears, | whose fur, on a cat, you might call calico'.

The Callimachean fragments, hymns, iambs and epigrams from

which these poems spring are referenced in the titles of each, though bracketed (e.g. '(Aetia, book 3, frag. 79)'), as if to self-efface; and single lines in the original Greek serve as epigraphs. Take, for instance, '(Epigram 56)', which reads in its totality:

τῶι με Κανωπίται Καλλίστιον εἴκοσι μύξαις

When I began writing, I felt like a constellation,
        some new fixture in the sky,
a lamp with twenty wicks, or at least
        an eternal flame. It was mostly a lie
I told myself, though a few of my friends bought into it. Now
        look at what I've become. I am, at best,
a slender candle under glass,
        a strip of magnesium you might
ignite for a demonstration in chemistry class,
        or else a meteorite, fast
becoming invisible, something you could point out
        to a child, a faint
impression, a line everyone knows can't last.

Only the first line of Callimachus's Epigram 56 is quoted by Burt, and the literal translation offered by the Loeb Classical Library offers the following:

τῶι με Κανωπίται Καλλίστιον εἴκοσι μύξαις
πλούσιον ἁ Κριτίου λύχνον ἔθηκε θεῶι
εὐξαμένα περὶ παιδὸς Ἀπελλίδος: ἐς δ᾽ ἐμὰ φέγγη
ἀθρήσας φάσεις Ἕσπερε πῶς ἔπεσεσ᾽.

To the god of Canopus did Callistion, daughter of Critias, dedicate me—a lamp enriched with twenty nozzles: a vow for her child Apellis. Looking on my light thou wilt say, "Hesperus, how art thou fallen?"

Fragments or short texts such as this offer fertile ground for adaptor-translators: the white space which surrounds the text (its brevity or concision the result of being broken up or worn down by time), becomes freighted with imaginative possibility. They offer much room for play to the poet-translator, and can become a study in the theory and practice of translation itself. As Mark Payne notes in the foreword, 'the translation brings out the truth of the original. It is the bloom of its hidden being.'

In playing with her source material in such a way, and particular in introducing anachronisms, Burt is in illustrious company. It is a tradition which stretches back at least as far as Agamemnon's helicopter in Christopher Logue's *War Music*, an 'account' of the *Iliad*. Anne Carson also comes to mind: the interview with 'Stesichoros' in *Autobiography of Red*, and the many liberties taken by that book with the fragments of Stesichorus's *Geryoneis*; or her latest work, *Norma Jeane Baker of Troy*. (And her more deadpan translations of Sappho's fragments in *If Not, Winter*, exemplify the potency of the white space which surrounds the fragment). This work of poetic contouring is like the shard of antique pottery, or the broken chips of fresco which have been reassembled in a museum, their gaps and missing pieces painted in, in an act of aesthetically-informed imagination. Except, in their work, we walk into the museum, only to find that in the artists' impression of an urn's missing remainder, Zeus is carrying a lightsabre, or licking an ice cream. The whole may be painted in an attic or archaic style, but with cheeky dares to spot the difference.

This can be read as an attempt to trouble our understanding of our relationship to the Classical: who, for starters, is the 'we' which presupposes an 'our'? The 'Classical' civilisations of Ancient Greece and Rome have, since the Early Modern period, been seen as the foundation of that punitive, paternalistic entity, 'Western civilisation', and, as such (and as the cultural site of a projected proto-whiteness), been used to enforce tactical notions of cultural hierarchy against the rest of the world. With her anachronisms, Burt is probing the presumed familiarity of the Classical period; making it uncanny, newly strange.

Where Burt best contributes to the tradition of classical reimaginings is in her undermining of some of its most tenacious bequests. In '(Epigram 33)', she unravels the persistently popular metaphor of love as a hunt in brief, blunt lines:

> Um, no.
> Love shouldn't work like that. If love is a hunt,
> it should be about who you want
> at your back, or by your side
> with dagger, chakram, trident or short bow,
> not what you string up in your larder.

There is enormous emancipatory potential here: we feel immediately loosed from millennia of toxic metaphor; the horizons of our imagination broadened. Burt has given us nothing less than a new way of conceptualising love. The most exquisite poem is the one which closes the collection. It departs from Callimachus's 'Hymn to Athena' (aka 'On the Bath of Pallas'), which radically reimagines the making of Tiresias ('the Eternal Trans of the Greek tradition', as Payne would have him). Tiresias is struck blind by Athena after he sees her bathing, but the poem's tour de force is Athena's piece of rhetoric in convincing her best friend (Tiresias's mother) that her curse is not cause for grief. 'Your son is your son, | he's right here, and he's going to live a long life, | ... because you love him, and because I have loved you'. With poems such as these, Burt designates new heirs of the Classical tradition, and we are wealthier for it.

Iberian Irony and Caribbean Confluences

Juana Adcock reviews *Ten Contemporary Spanish Women Poets*,
edited and translated by Terence Dooley, Shearsman books, 2020
The Sea Needs No Ornament/ El mar no necesita ornamento, edited
and translated by Loretta Collins Klobah and Marieta Grau Perejoan,
Peepal Press, 2020

Ten Contemporary Spanish Women Poets is the first anthology to bring
into the English language an all-female cast of contemporary
Spanish poets. Female poets have traditionally been relegated to the
background in the male-dominated and often actively misogynist
scene that is poetry in Spain, where one important figure in
publishing recently even went so far as to write in an *El Mundo*
cultural supplement that 'Women's poetry doesn't bear comparison
to men's. There wasn't an important woman poet in the whole of
the twentieth century and there isn't one now.' The poetry world
in Spain has a long way to go in terms of the gender gap: Spain's
national poetry award has been awarded 52 times, and only 4 times
to women – a fact that lends Terence Dooley's anthology particular
urgency.

The selected poets navigate evolving gender roles in a post-
dictatorship, post-financial crash Spain, in which the dreams of
neoliberalism have been shattered. Mercedes Cebrián needles the
vacuousness of life for salaried women of the Easyjet generation:
'I represent modernity: look | at my fillings, they're quality. The
girl | who did them for me is younger than you and just off | for a
fun weekend in Copenhagen.' Cebrián also takes on the shifting
shadow of the dictatorship:

Everything is Franco's fault – it has a ring to it,
so I say it again now the daylight
is less bleak. Anyway, how many feminists
does it take to change a light-bulb?
No-one told Franco that sort of joke.
I can picture his baffled expression
as he listened, and, nevertheless,
those jokes are also Franco's fault.

In 'Poverty seen from Europe', Julieta Valero speaks of 'mother nature but father market,' and as the poets in this anthology ponder on how to exist in this world which is largely unstable, there seems to be a particular emphasis on how the economy shapes the world of intimate relationships and with it, a sense of self. Martha Asunción Alonso writes 'The metro reached our suburb | too late. | Our escape plans were already laid.' Many of the poets attempt what Bertha García Faet explains is a subversion of what women's writing is expected to do: 'to be romantic and talk about my body,' but doing it 'to such an extreme, that I explode the stereotype.'

Dooley's translations recreate the original voices in a credible and accurate way, without homogenising the diction. The anthology includes only poets working in Castilian Spanish, to the unacknowledged exclusion of the other languages of Spain such as Catalan, Valencian, Mallorcan, Galician and Basque, but Arc has given us these language-specific anthologies relatively recently.

The Sea Needs No Ornament/ El mar no necesita ornamento (Peepal Press) is a mesmerising bilingual anthology of 33 contemporary Caribbean women poets, edited and translated by scholars Loretta Collins Klobah and Marieta Grau Perejoan. The anthology brings together poets from the Caribbean territories and their diasporas working in English and Spanish, and while poetry in other Caribbean languages (such as French, Hindustani, Dutch, Papiamento, creoles and endangered indigenous languages) could not be included, the selection is extensive enough to give a sense of the kind of poetry being written in this border-transcending region. As the editors explain, 'our project intends to encourage plurilingual abilities, collaboration and communication or the ability to speak to each other.' Placed in alphabetical rather than geographical order, English and Spanish-speaking poets are side by side, revealing confluences and commonalities, and sharing a kind of language that goes beyond the linguistic – in the words of the Trinidad-based poet Jennifer Rahim, 'a language playing dead only | to ambush change.'

Whether in San Juan, Madrid, Havana, Manchester, Santo Domingo or Leeds, we can see how the violence and decadence of the city seeps into the poets' consciousness as the place where, in the words of Cuban Gelsys García Lorenzo 'Imperialism is a gum | vending machine.' Nicole Cecilia Delgado writes: 'I've lost my innocence in this city | I recognize the signs of war in the stop lights | better to live between walls that tremble from kiss to kiss | than to count bullet scars on the windows.' Or, in Thaís Espaillat: 'the rain, wanting to be a good citizen, | looks for a garbage can | but it doesn't find one, | so it fills the street | with Tetra packs | and plastic bags | and pink leaflets that speak of the | Apocalypse'.

There is also a preoccupation with violence against women. Zulema Gutiérrez Lozano writes that 'Sofía is a red stain the highway absorbs like a tattoo,' while in Jamila Medina Ríos's visionary, linguistically playful poetry 'the woman sharpens the filigree of her madness | sex her sex her sex her | close   open   saw [...] the mother extracted from the whore.' In Tiphanie Yanique, 'the island | is a woman, therefore | dangerous things live below'. In this context, Vahni Capildeo's reflections on soucouyants and home burn with the same flame: 'Fireball shedding her skin bloodkisses not just cattle |

Her stored skin poisoned by raging neighbours with stamped thighs |
She puts on a skin that smelts her, woman of no return.' Donna Aza
Weir-Soley writes of 'lugging the same old loads | avoiding the same
cracks | (that broke our mothers' backs)', which resonates with
Malika Booker's:

> My mother knows pain
> a sorrowful gospel type of pain
> a slowly losing her eyesight,
> eye drops every night pain
> a headache worrying for her children overseas,
> praying for their safety pain,
> a stare through each night, eyes blackening,
> hope they are alright pain.

All of these authors take on, in the words of Jamila Medina Ríos, 'the
exercise of writing like a whiplash in the flesh,' and the editors tackle
the gargantuan challenge of translating such a range of voices in
both directions between English and Spanish with authority and skill,
working closely with the poets themselves. The anthology sets a
precedent in particular when rendering the specificities of Caribbean
English syntax into Spanish, which has not often been done before,
a fact further complicated by colloquial Caribbean Spanish not
being represented as distinctly in poetry, so there are not many
literary conventions for a translator to rely on.

NOTES ON CONTRIBUTORS

JUANA ADCOCK is a Latinx poet, translator and performer working in English and Spanish. Her English-language debut, *Split* (Blue Diode Press) was awarded the Poetry Book Society Winter Choice in 2019.

YOSANO AKIKO (1878–1942) is a prominent figure in twentieth-century Japanese poetry: a prolific writer known for her passionate tanka, social criticism, and translation of *The Tale of Genji* into modern Japanese.

ALI AL-JAMRI is a Bahraini British poet and writer. He is a participant of the 2020 BBC Words First talent programme and one of his stories was a notable contender in the Bristol Short Story Prize.

ABU AL-QASSIM AL-SHABBI (1909–1934) is Tunisia's national poet, best known for his poems 'The Desire of Life' and 'To the Tyrants of the World', which became emblems of the Arab Uprisings in the 2010s. He died aged 25 of chronic heart illness.

LILY ARNOLD is a Leeds based artist. Sometimes she does huge paintings on big walls, and sometimes she does tiny drawings in small zines. Lily likes watching garden birds and eating pizza.

BEBE ASHLEY lives in Belfast and is interested in linguistic and ekphrastic translations. Her debut collection, *Gold Light Shining*, was published by Banshee Press this year. www.bebe-ashley.com

NASIM REBECCA ASL is a Glasgow-based poet and journalist. Her work has been published in multiple magazines and her poem 'Nemidoonam' was featured in the inaugural Fringe of Colour Films.

CLAUDIA BERRUETO was born in 1978. She is a poet from Saltillo, in the north of Mexico. A fellow of the Foundation for Mexican Literature, and National Fund for Culture and Arts, her collection, *Polvo doméstico* (Domestic Dust), won the national prize of poetry in Tijuana in 2009. Her latest collection is *Sesgo* (Bias).

BHĀVAKADEVĪ was a poet living probably sometime between the seventh and eleventh centuries AD, writing in Sanskrit.

S. CORINNA BILLE (1912–1979) was a French-speaking Swiss writer whose work includes novels, short stories, and prose poems. She won the Schiller Prize and the Prix Goncourt de la Nouvelle.

NATALIE LINH BOLDERSTON is a Vietnamese-Chinese-British poet. She won a 2020 Eric Gregory Award and her pamphlet, *The Protection of Ghosts*, is published with V. Press.

ZOË BRIGLEY has three poetry collections: *Hand & Skull, Conquest*, and *The Secret* (Bloodaxe), plus a chapbook forthcoming: *Aubade After a French Movie* (Broken Sleep), including translations of Gwerful Mechain.

KATIE BYFORD is a poet and filmmaker with work published in anthologies by Bloodaxe and Macmillan. She received Durham University's Maltby Exhibition Prize for her dissertation on Sappho translation.

JAMES BYRNE is a poet, editor and translator living near Liverpool. He is Reader in Contemporary Literature at Edge Hill University and co-edited *I am a Rohingya: Poetry from the Camps and Beyond* (Arc, 2019), a PBS World Choice.

MATTHEW CALEY's debut *Thirst* was nominated for The Forward Prize for best first collection. He has since published five more collections, most recently *Trawlerman's Turquoise*. He gave the StAnza Lecture 2020.

CLAIRE CARLOTTI is studying English at Cambridge University, and has been writing a mixture of (unpublished) short stories and poetry for several years in her spare time. This is her first published translation.

ILHAN SAMI ÇOMAK is a Turkish poet who has been in prison there for 26 years.

SHEILA CUSSONS (1922–2004) was a visual artist and prize-winning poet who wrote in Afrikaans. She lived in Europe for several decades before returning to her native South Africa in 1983.

JADE CUTTLE is Arts Commissioning Editor at *The Times*. She has written poetry for the BBC and *The Spectator*, and released an album of poem-songs *Algal Bloom* through Warren Records. www.jadecuttle.com

ELLA DUFFY's debut pamphlet, *New Hunger*, was published by Smith|Doorstop in May 2020. Her upcoming pamphlet, *Rootstalk*, will be published by Hazel Press in November 2020.

ENHEDUANNA was a high priestess from ancient Mesopotamia and the first poet in recorded history.

PATRICIA ESTEBAN was born in Madrid in 1975, and is a poet and an academic. She teaches Spanish American literature in Madrid. Her publications include the collection *El rescate invisible* (Amargord, 2005).

PARVIN ETESAMI (1907–1941) was a poet whose work was ground-breaking in its content, themes and use of classical forms of Persian poetry.

SUZANNAH EVANS lives in Sheffield. Her pamphlet *Confusion Species* was a winner in the 2012 Poetry Business Competition and her debut collection is *Near Future* (Nine Arches, 2018).

MARILYN HACKER is the author of fourteen books of poems, including *Blazons* (Carcanet, 2019) and eighteen collections of translations. She lives in Paris.

ROSANNA HILDYARD is a writer, editor and translator from North Yorkshire. Her translation of Alfred Jarry, *Ubu Trump,* was published in 2016.

GUNVOR HOFMO (1921–1995) published twenty poetry collections over 48 years, with distinct styles before and after a sixteen-year silent period. All of Hofmo's work is published by Gyldendal Norsk Forlag.

HÒ XUÂN HƯƠNG was a Vietnamese poet born in the late eighteenth century in Nghệ An Province. She is believed to have grown up in Thăng Long (now Hanoi).

AINEE JEONG graduated with a B.A. in English from Emory University and received her M.A. in English with a Certificate in Literary Translation from the University of Connecticut.

HWANG JINI (1506–1560) was a kisaeng during Korea's Joseon Dynasty. She was also known by her kisaeng name Myeongwol, meaning 'bright moon'.

YUI KAJITA is an early-career scholar of English literature, a Japanese-English translator, and an aspiring illustrator. She completed her PhD on Hardy and de la Mare at the University of Cambridge.

MASCHA KALÉKO (1907–1975) was a Polish-German-Jewish poet born in Galicia (now part of Ukraine). After publishing two successful volumes celebrating and satirizing urban life in the late Weimar Republic, Kaléko was forced into exile, thereafter spending her life in the USA and Israel.

LISA KATZ is the translator of *The Absolute Reader*, a chapbook of verse by Miri Ben Simhon (Toad Press 2020) and books by poets Admiel Kosman, Agi Mishol and Tuvia Ruebner.

KATIE KIRKPATRICK studies French at the University of Oxford. She won the 12–18 category of the BBC Proms Poetry Competition 2019 and is a commended Foyle Young Poet.

KAREN LEEDER is an academic, writer and translator of modern German poetry, most recently Ulrike Almut Sandig, *I am a field of oil-seed rape give cover to deer and shine like thirteen oil-paintings piled one on top of the other* (Seagull Books, 2020).

FEDERICO GARCÍA LORCA (1898–1936) was a Spanish poet and playwright.

CLARA MARINO is a Japanese-English translator and a scholar of Japanese studies. She is currently pursuing an MA at the University of Massachusetts Amherst.

KEVIN MAYNARD taught English for many decades. Retirement has enabled him to concentrate on translation. His translations of ancient and medieval Chinese war poetry were published as *The Iron Flute* (Arc, 2019). He was twice commended in the Stephen Spender Competition.

GWERFUL MECHAIN (ca. 1460–1502) was a medieval Welsh poet, who wrote in Cymraeg, and left a substantial body of work, witty and erotic in content. Mechain was talented at writing strict Welsh forms.

SELMA MEERBAUM-EISINGER (1924–1942) was a Romanian-born, German-speaking poet, who died aged 18 in the Michailowka labour camp. Her collection, *Blütenlese,* was rediscovered and published by Tel Aviv University Press in 1979.

ALEX MEPHAM is a PhD student investigating how background noise impacts speech understanding. Previously living throughout Scandinavia, Alex takes interest in contemporary Nordic literature. Alex currently lives in York.

MICHÈLE MÉTAIL is a minimalist poet, performer, artist and a scholar of ancient Chinese verse forms. Her acclaimed anthology of Chinese reversible poems, *Wild Geese Returning*, was published in English in 2017 in a translation by Jody Gladding.

HACHIKAI MIMI (1974–) is a prominent voice in Japanese poetry. Her debut collection won the Nakahara Chuya Prize, and since then she has been a prolific writer of poetry, fiction, essays, and reviews. Her fifth collection *Kao wo arau mizu* won the Ayukawa Nobuo Prize.

HELEN MORT is a poet and fiction writer based in Sheffield. She has published two pamphlets with tall-lighthouse press and two full length collections with Chatto & Windus, *Division Street* (2013) and *No Map Could Show Them* (2016).

VICTORIA MOUL lives in London where she teaches and writes mainly about Latin and English poetry. She has a long-standing interest in Sanskrit literature.

KATRINA NAOMI's latest collection, *Wild Persistence*, (Seren) was published in June 2020. Her poetry has appeared on Radio 4's *Front Row* and on Poems on the Underground. Katrina is learning Kernewek (Cornish).

HELGA M. NOVAK, also Maria Karlsdottir (1935–2013), was a German-Icelandic writer who grew up in East Germany. She wrote seven major collections of poetry. Schöffling and Co. published her complete poems *So lange noch Liebesbriefe eintreffen* in 1999.

MÀIRI MHÒR NAN ÒRAN (Màiri MacPherson), 1821–1898, was an oral, political poet and lyricist who was born and died in Skye. Her work focused largely on the Highland Clearances.

JENNY O'SULLIVAN is a writer, comic artist and drag performer from Huddersfield. Having studied languages, they now work as a curatorial trainee in Leicester and translate for a German gallery.

JULIA ANASTASIA PELOSI-THORPE translates into English and into XML (TEI). Her translations of Italian and Latin poetry are published in the *Journal of Italian Translation, Griffith Review, Asymptote, Los Angeles Review, Oberon Poetry,* and more.

NADĚŽDA PLÍŠKOVÁ was a twentieth century Czech poet, sculptor and graphic artist.

GISELE PRASSINOS (1920–2015) was a French-speaking surrealist poet of Greek and Turkish heritage. Her first book was *La Sauterelle arthritique* (The Arthritic Grasshopper).

VAUGHAN RAPATAHANA (Te Ātiawa) is widely published across several genre in both his main languages, te reo Māori and English and his work has been translated into Bahasa Malaysia, Italian, French and Mandarin.

CHRISTA REINIG (1926–2008) was a feminist, lesbian poet and author. Her career began in East Berlin, where her works were later banned after being published in West Germany.

FAHMIDA RIAZ was a Pakistani poet, translator and human rights activist who published over 15 books of fiction and poetry. She passed away in 2018.

SAPPHO (or Psappha), a lyric poet, probably lived during the 6th century BC on the ancient Greek island of Lesbos. She is famous for composing erotic poetry about other women.

ANKITA SAXENA is a poet and playwright based in London. She is part of the Octavia Collective of womxn of colour poets and a former Barbican Young Poet.

RYAN SCOTT's translation of Jiří Kolář's collection *A User's Manual* was released by Twisted Spoon Press.

LOUISA SIEFERT was one of the most successful French female poets of the nineteenth century. Her first collection, *Rayons perdus* (1868), sold-out, and she published several further collections.

YVETTE SIEGERT is a Latinx poet and translator, and currently a Clarendon Scholar reading for a DPhil in Medieval and Modern Languages at Merton College, Oxford.

ŚĪLABHATTĀRIKĀ was a poet living probably sometime between the seventh and eleventh centuries AD, writing in Sanskrit.

MIRI BEN SIMHON (1950–1996) was born in Marseille to Moroccan parents on their way to Israel. In 2018 her collected poems were republished in Hebrew. In 2020 a chapbook, *The Absolute Reader*, appeared in English (Toad Press).

SUHRAB SIRAT is an exiled poet, writer, journalist, and former civil society activist from Afghanistan. His first booklet of poetry in English will be published later this year by Exiled Writers Ink.

NOÉMIA DE SOUSA was a Mozambican poet and journalist. Widely published and read, she's considered a leading African poet. Noémia is the author of *Negro Sangue* (2001), edited by the Mozambican Writers Association.

CAROLINE STOCKFORD is a poet and translator working in the field of human rights and freedom of expression in Turkey. She was one of the editors and translators of Haydar Ergülen's poetry in English, *Pomegranate Garden*.

FADWA SULEIMAN was born in Aleppo in 1970. Her collection of poems, كلّما بلع القم (As The Moon Rose), was published in 2013. She died of cancer in Paris in 2017.

SULPICIA is understood today to have been a Roman elegist of the late first century BCE. One of the rare female voices in Latin poetry, her six extant poems were discovered within the Corpus Tibullianum, long thought the work of male contemporary poet Tibullus.

STEPHANIE SY-QUIA is a freelance writer and critic based in London. Her writing has been featured in *The Poetry Review, Poetry London, The TLS*, and others. She is a member of the Ledbury Emerging Poetry Critics Programme.

PHILIP TERRY was born in Belfast, and is a poet and translator. He is currently translating Ice Age signs from the caves at Lascaux. *The Penguin Book of Oulipo,* which he edited, appeared in 2019.

SHASH TREVETT is a Tamil from Sri Lanka. She is currently co-editing, along with Vidyan Ravinthiran and Seni Seneviratne, an anthology of Tamil, Sinhala and English poetry from Sri Lanka and related diasporas.

MARINA TSVETAEVA was born in Moscow and her life coincided with some of the most turbulent years in Russian history. At 18 she published her first collection of poems, *Evening Album*. She also wrote verse plays and prose.

SUE VICKERMAN's published translations include *Kathrin Schmidt: Twenty Poems* (Arc, 2020) and poems in *The Poetry Review* and *Stockholm Review*. Her translation of Schmidt's story collection will be published in 2021. suevickerman.eu

VIDYĀ was a poet living probably sometime between the seventh and eleventh centuries AD, writing in Sanskrit.

ANDREW VAN DER VLIES is a South African-born writer educated at the University of Oxford. He is currently professor of contemporary literature at Queen Mary University of London.

JAMES WOMACK teaches Spanish and Russian translation at Cambridge University. He has published three collections of poems, most recently *Homunculus* (2020), as well as versions of Mayakovsky, Tvardovsky and Manuel Vilas.

JESSICA WOOD is a British poet based in Lisbon. Her poems are excavations of the question 'what does it mean to be human?'

NAI XIAN was one of several non-Han poets who rose to prominence during the Yuan dynasty (1271–1368). He belonged to the Karluk nomadic people, though he grew up within China. He died in an army camp far from home.

KYOKO YOSHIDA (1969–) writes fiction in English and translates from/ into Japanese. Her story collections are *Disorientalism* (Vagabond Press) and *Spring Sleepers* (Strangers Press). She teaches American Literature at Ritsumeikan University.

BELINDA ZHAWI is a Zimbabwean writer and author of *Small Inheritances* (ignitionpress, 2018) and co-founder of BORN::FREE. Belinda experiments with sound as MA.MOYO – she's been featured on platforms including Boiler Room, BBC Radio, & Worldwide FM.